ABOUT THE AI

D1621720

F. P. (Tony) Bennett's love of birds — especially tropical species — is rooted in the Lower Rio Grande Valley of Texas.

A resident of the southern tip of the Lone Star State since boyhood, Bennett has also traveled extensively in Mexico, Central and South America. His travels have given him the chance to see with his own eyes many of the colorful species he has come to draw and paint.

His work appears in "A Field Guide to the Birds of Mexico and Central America," published by The University of Texas Press, and has been included in the Leigh Yawkey Woodson Art Museum's annual "Birds in Art" exhibit, the most prestigious event of its kind.

Bennett, who lives in Harlingen, is currently at work on a book that will feature his full-color illustration of the world's 320-plus hummingbird species, along with their native habitats and many of the flowers on which they feed.

CONTRIBUTORS

We thank all those people who so generously contributed recipes for our collection. We apologize if we have inadvertently omitted any name of a contributor or tester. In some instances recipes were combined or adapted after extensive testing. Friends and family were particularly helpful testers.

Carin Adams	Holly S. Fuller	Cindy Robinson
Colleen Albury	Ginny K. Gibson	Carrie Lee Rowe
Jodie Allex	J.L. Gipson	Nadine Salinas
Tanya Anderson	Patty Gorges	Ola Sandlin
Carla Armstrong	Mickey Graham	Laura Schauer
Deanna Baird	Gene Graham	Rita Scoggins
Joe Baldwin	Annette Grayson	Beverly Searle
Ellen Ballenger	Debra F. Groves	Roxie Shimotsu
Olga D. Barron	Carolyn Hall	Julie Sullivan Siller
Louise Batot	Bridget Henderson	Mary Beth Simmons
Patrick Bauer	Lynne Hendrix	Laurie Simmons
Lisa Bellamy	Dorothy Padilla Hinojosa	Lisa Spanihel
Doris & Russell Bentley	Pam Holmes	Liz Spates
Cathy Binney	Cara Horne	Susan Stapleton
Anita Boswell	Frances Hury	Laura Surovic
Monica Burdette	Joan Jones	Marty Tapp
Lorraine Burns	Terry Kane	Sue Ann Taubert
Betty H. Cass	Gwen Keeling	Jane Theriot
Allan Cass	Ann Kwiatkowski	Lisa Tichenor
Eleanor Binney Childress	Janice Labar	Cookie Tisdale
Jane Clark	Lillian Lamon	Darlene Topp
Dixie Coleman	Nan Lawler	Norma Tout
Julie Cook	Dena Levine	Jimmie Traylor
Gretchen Cooley	Mary C. Lewis	Kelli Trevino
Nancy Crockett	Sandra Lopez	Kelly Trolinger
Linda Cruz	Jeannie Mackie	Bill & Lisa Turner
Cary Curtis	Nancy Maggard	Maria Uecker
Tommy Curtis	Eileen Marshall	Katherine Uhlhorn
Charlotte Dahm	Mary Joy Mason	Deborah Vann
LaVerne Daley	Mona Mason	Alayne Villarreal
Dee Davis	Trudi Mayo	Linda Wade
Catherine Davis	Mary Sharp Mount	Shaun Wadkins
Paula DeBolt	Betty Mungia	Pamela Warren
Cathy Drummond	Deanna Murphy	Sandy Wheeler
Mary Katherine Duffy	Sharon Reynolds Norris	Drenda Wiley
Monica Dunkin	Holly Omick	Denise Williams
La Donna Easley	Jiske Ong	Tina Wilson
Stacy Ehrlich	Kay Owens	William Worley
Amy Ehrlich	Karen Pinkerton	Debe Wright
Robin Farris	Amy Plum	Dorothy Yarbrough
Helen Feldman	Judy Quisenberry	Nancy Yates
Elsie A. Fisher	Norma Rabb	Betty Youker
Jim Fitzgerald	Patti Reeves	Teri Youngblood
Marjorie Flory	Kim Reynolds	Teri Zamora
Traci Forman	Dolly Robbins	Patti Zimny

Rio Riches

Recipes Celebrating the Rich Natural Diversity of the Rio Grande Valley

The Junior League of Harlingen, Inc.
Harlingen, Texas

The Junior League of Harlingen, Inc. is an organization of women committed to promoting voluntarism and to improving the community through the effective action and leadership of trained volunteers. Its purpose is exclusively educational and charitable.

For information on purchasing
additional copies please write or call:

The Junior League of Harlingen, Inc.
P. O. Box 1726
Harlingen, Texas 78551
210.425.5690
Email: rioriches@harlingen.juniorleague.org
http: harlingen.junior league.org/harlingen/

ISBN: 0-9656487-0-2

Printed in the USA by

WIMMER
The Wimmer Companies, Inc.
Memphis

INTRODUCTION

In this land of subtle beauty where the Rio Grande prepares to meet the glittering Gulf of Mexico, we find ourselves at home.

Close to Mexico, and separated – it sometimes seems – from the rest of Texas, we have built a special place here amongst the huisache and wild olive, the prickly pear and palms. It is a place of rich diversity in culture and in nature, where the pace is easy, the people are welcoming in two languages and where hospitality is practiced – however humble or refined – from the heart.

We call our corner of the world "The Valley," and we celebrate the unique advantages of living in this special place.

A raucous crowd of red-headed parrots perched in the tree tops. A luxuriant banner of purple bougainvillea framing a gateway, the jewel-like colors of a hummingbird outside a kitchen window.

Fields for the sportsman, the Laguna Madre and beyond for the fishermen, endless South Padre Island beaches for our children, and the weather to enjoy them year-round – these are but a few of the reasons why we have come, and stayed.

In our homes as well, we celebrate the richness of this land beside the grand river.

Our kitchens are scented with garlic, lime and cilantro. Our recipes feature ingredients – world-famous grapefruit, sweet onions, red peppers and other delights – fresh from the fields of the "Magic Valley." Our menus combine the best of Mexico and Texas into a cuisine all its own.

Far from banquet halls and big city caterers, entertaining – whether extravagant or simple – becomes and art form that is relaxed, intimate – and a true reflection of personal style. Special days often are celebrated around the grill, with wild game stalked through the South Texas brushland, or red snapper plucked fresh from the Gulf. Parties can be group affairs – combining the talents of many hostesses who are also friends. On a cool fall evening or a warm spring night, a pot luck supper becomes a neighborhood feast where one more guest is always welcome.

The Harlingen Junior League is made up of dedicated women from many walks of life, who gladly support their community and each other. We are proud to present this special collection of recipes, double-tested with care, from our kitchens to yours. The proceeds of this cookbook, a major fund-raiser for the league, will go toward improving the lives of women and children in our community.

Through the pages of "Rio Riches," we welcome you into our homes, and we offer you our best. SALUD!

By Karen Hastings Pinkerton
Karen is a newspaper journalist and freelance writer who joined the Harlingen Junior League in 1995.

Alta Mira Oriole

TABLE OF CONTENTS

Sombrero signifies recipes translated in Spanish.

Clock signifies recipes that are quick and easy.

Feather signifies recipes which are lighter fare.

ACKNOWLEDGEMENTS

Rio Riches
Cookbook Committee
1994-1997

Debe Wright - *Co-Chairman*
Teri Youngblood - *Co-Chairman*
Mary Katherine Duffy - *Word Processing*

Julie Cook	Kim Johnson
Karen Pinkerton	Kim Reynolds
Rosemary Slagle	Marty Tapp
Norma Tout	Maria Uecker

Research & Planning

Anita Boswell	Gemma Cantu
Shelley Cocke	Benzi Craig
Ginny Gibson	Debbie Groves
Traci Forman	Wanda Garcia
Abby Gonzalez	Laura Gonzalez
Mary Klement	Lillian Lamon
Eileen Marshall	Sharon Norris
Cindy Robinson	Kelli Treviño
Christie Hirst	

Sustaining Advisors

Donna Bonner	Lynne Hendrix
Kay Owens	Pam Smith

Presidents

Lillian Lamon 93-94	Ellen Ballenger 94-95
Cindy Robinson 95-96	Pam Holmes 96-97

Cookbook Title
Debe Wright

Graphic Design
The Graphics Center, Harlingen

Historical Coordinator
Donna Bonner

Contributing Artist
E. P. (Tony) Bennett

Editing and Proofreading Assistance

Lynne Hendrix	Kay Owens
June Motheral	

Appetizers & Drinks

TEXAS CAVIAR

3	tomatoes, chopped
5-6	cherry peppers, de-seeded and chopped
3-4	green onions, chopped
1	small can chopped black olives
3	tablespoons oil
1 ½	teaspoons vinegar
1	can black-eyed peas
1	teaspoon garlic salt
	salsa to taste

Mix all ingredients. Chill three to four hours. Serve with tortilla chips.

Yield: 24 servings

SOUTHWESTERN CHEESECAKE

1	cup tortilla chips, finely crushed
3	tablespoons margarine, melted
2	(8-ounce) packages cream cheese, softened
2	eggs
1	(8-ounce) package Colby/Monterey Jack cheese, shredded
1	(4-ounce) can chopped green chilis, drained
1	cup sour cream
1	cup yellow or orange bell pepper, chopped
½	cup green onion, chopped
⅓	cup tomatoes, chopped
¼	cup pitted ripe olive slices

Heat oven to 325°. Stir chips and margarine in small bowl and press onto bottom of 9-inch springform pan. Bake 15 minutes. In a large mixing bowl, beat cream cheese and eggs at medium speed until well blended. Mix in shredded cheese and green chilis. Pour over crust and bake 30 minutes. When finished baking, spread sour cream over cheesecake and refrigerate. Before serving, loosen cake sides and remove rim of pan. Top with remaining ingredients just before serving.

Yield: 16-20 servings

PARTY CHILE-CHEESE APPETIZERS

10	eggs
½	cup flour
1	teaspoon baking powder
⅛	teaspoon salt
½	cup butter or margarine, melted
1	(8-ounce) can chopped green chilis
1	pint cottage cheese
1	pound Monterey Jack cheese, shredded

Beat eggs slightly. Blend in flour, baking powder and salt. Add melted butter, green chilis and cheeses and mix just enough to blend. Spread batter in greased 9 x 13-inch glass baking dish. Bake at 400° for 15 minutes. Reduce heat to 350° and bake an additional 35 to 40 minutes. Cut into bite-size squares. Serve on small square crackers or tostado.

Yield: 60-100 one-inch squares.

SPINACH STRATA

54	round buttery crackers
2	(10-ounce) packages frozen chopped spinach
1 ½	cups Muenster cheese, shredded
2 ½	cups milk
5	eggs
2	tablespoons Dijon mustard
½	teaspoon hot pepper sauce
1	teaspoon garlic powder (not garlic salt)

In 3-quart baking dish, arrange 18 crackers in three long rows. Combine spinach and two cups shredded cheese. Spoon half of mixture over crackers. Repeat layers. Top with remaining crackers and sprinkle with remaining cheese. In medium bowl, beat together milk, eggs, mustard, pepper sauce and garlic powder. Pour evenly over spinach mixture in baking dish. Refrigerate one hour. Bake at 350° for one hour or until puffed and golden. Cut into squares to serve.

Yield: 12 large or 24 small servings

BBQ PORCUPINE BALLS

3	pounds ground beef
1	(12-ounce) can evaporated milk
1	cup oatmeal
1	cup cracker crumbs
2	eggs
½	cup onion, chopped
½	teaspoon garlic powder
2	teaspoons salt
½	teaspoon pepper
2	teaspoons chili powder

Sauce:

2	cups catsup
1	cup brown sugar
½	teaspoon liquid smoke
½	teaspoon garlic powder
¼	cup onion, chopped

To make meatballs, combine all ingredients and shape into soft, walnut-sized balls. Place in a single layer on wax paper lined cookie sheets and freeze until solid. Store frozen meatballs in freezer bags until ready to cook. To make sauce, combine sauce ingredients and stir until sugar is dissolved. Place frozen meatballs in a 9 x 13-inch baking dish and cover thoroughly with sauce. Bake at 350° for one hour.

Yield: 80 meatballs

White-tailed Kite

ASPARAGUS HERB CREPES

Crepes:
1 ½ cups all-purpose flour, sifted
1 cup milk
1 cup water
4 eggs
pinch of salt
pinch of nutmeg, freshly grated
½ stick unsalted butter, melted
1 tablespoon fresh flat leaf parsley, finely minced
1 tablespoon fresh chives, finely minced
1 tablespoon fresh dill, finely minced
1 teaspoon butter

Filling:
1 pound Brie cheese, rind removed
4 ounces Roquefort cheese
6 tablespoons unsalted butter, room temperature
½ cup whipping cream
freshly ground white pepper
20-25 fresh asparagus spears, steamed and chilled

Translated on page 240

Combine flour, milk, water, eggs, salt and nutmeg in a blender and mix until smooth. Pour into mixing bowl. Add melted butter and herbs and whisk until blended. Cover and let stand two hours at room temperature for flavors to combine. Heat one teaspoon of butter in a six-inch crepe pan. Add just enough batter to coat the bottom of the pan and lightly brown crepe on each side. Repeat with remaining batter, adding more butter as necessary.

In a food processor, combine cheeses and butter in bowl and mix using six on/off turns. Add cream and pepper and blend until completely smooth. Cover and let stand at room temperature one hour before serving.

To assemble crepes, place an asparagus spear in the center of each crepe. Put the filling in a pastry bag and pipe the filling down the side of the asparagus. Roll crepe like a tortilla.

Yield: 20 servings

ARTICHOKE BITES

2 (6-ounce) jars marinated
  artichoke hearts
1 small onion, chopped
2 cloves garlic, minced
4 eggs
¼ cup dry Italian flavored
  bread crumbs
⅛ teaspoon black pepper
⅛ teaspoon oregano
2 cups sharp Cheddar cheese,
  shredded
2 tablespoons fresh parsley

Drain juice of artichokes in frying pan. Chop artichokes and set aside. Sauté onions and garlic in frying pan until onion is translucent, about five minutes. Add artichokes and mix well. In a bowl, beat eggs. Add bread crumbs, pepper, and oregano. Stir in cheese, parsley and artichoke mixture. Turn into an 11-inch shallow pan. Bake at 325° for 30 minutes. Cool. Cut in squares.

Yield: 6 dozen squares

STUFFED MUSHROOMS

18-20 mushrooms
6 scallions, finely chopped
1 tablespoon garlic, minced
3 tablespoons butter
3 tablespoons sun-dried tomatoes,
  drained and finely minced
3 tablespoons fine dry bread
  crumbs
6 tablespoons Parmesan cheese,
  freshly grated
  salt and pepper to taste

Clean mushrooms and separate the stems from the caps. Finely chop the stems and sauté with scallions and garlic in butter until stems are tender. Stir in tomatoes, bread crumbs and three tablespoons of cheese. Salt and pepper to taste. Place the mushrooms in a lightly greased shallow baking dish. Divide the mixture among the caps and mound slightly. Sprinkle with the remaining parmesan cheese. Bake at 400° until heated through and cheese is golden brown.

Yield: 18-20 mushrooms

BLUE CHEESE WAFERS

2	(4-ounce) packages blue cheese, crumbled
1	stick butter, softened
1 ⅓	cups flour
¾	cup pecans, finely chopped
1	teaspoon ground red pepper

Beat blue cheese and butter with an electric mixer until fluffy. Blend in flour, pecans and red pepper. Shape dough into two logs about eight to nine inches long. Cover with wax paper and refrigerate two or three hours until firm. Cut each log into 1/4-inch slices and place on ungreased cookie sheets. Bake at 350° for 13 to 15 minutes or until golden brown. Carefully transfer to wire racks.

Yield: 5-6 dozen

SORRENTO'S STUFFED BREAD

2	large French bread loaves
6	slices bacon, cooked
1	(12-ounce) package Swiss cheese slices
2	bunches green onions, chopped
2	sticks butter, sliced

Translated on page 241

Slice bread in half lengthwise, but do not cut all the way through. Place all ingredients between slices, except one stick of butter. Use the remaining stick of butter on top of bread. Wrap in foil and bake at 350° for 20 minutes or until cheese has melted.

Yield: 16 servings

BACON & CHEESE SANDWICH SPREAD

1   pound bacon, cooked, crumbled
     and cooled
2   cups Cheddar cheese, shredded
½   cup sliced almonds, toasted
1   cup mayonnaise
2   tablespoons green onions,
     chopped
16   slices white or wheat sandwich
     bread

Translated on page 241

Mix all ingredients and blend well. Spread on bread and make a sandwich. Cut off crusts and cut into quarters to serve.

Yield: 32 servings

CURRIED CHEESE PATE WITH CHUTNEY

3   (8-ounce) packages cream
     cheese, softened
2   (10-ounce) packages sharp
     Cheddar cheese, shredded
2   teaspoons curry powder
½   teaspoon salt
¼   cup dry sherry
1   cup chutney, chopped
¼   cup green onion, chopped

Line a 7 x 6-inch, 2-quart dish with waxed paper. In large bowl, combine cream cheese, Cheddar cheese, curry powder, salt and sherry. With electric mixer or food processor, beat at medium speed until smooth. Turn into prepared dish and refrigerate, covered, until firm (at least four hours.)

To serve, loosen sides with spatula. Turn out into serving dish and remove waxed paper. Spread chutney on top and sprinkle green onions around edge. Let stand at room temperature 30 minutes before serving. Surround with small crackers.

Yield: 48 servings

KATY'S FISH DIP

2   cups cooked white fish, mashed
1   (8-ounce) package cream cheese, softened
3   teaspoons horseradish
2   teaspoons Worcestershire sauce
2   tablespoons hot pepper sauce
2   teaspoons onion, grated
1   teaspoon lemon juice
4   serrano peppers, finely chopped (can also use jalapeños)

Mix all ingredients and blend well. Shape on a platter and serve with crackers. Freezes well.

Yield: 8-10 servings

HOT ARTICHOKE & SALMON SPREAD

1   (14-ounce) can artichoke hearts, drained and finely chopped
2   cups mayonnaise
2   cups Parmesan cheese, freshly grated
1 ½ cups canned salmon, drained and picked through*
½   teaspoon hot pepper sauce
½   cup toasted almonds (optional) parsley for garnish

Combine artichoke hearts, mayonnaise, cheese, salmon and hot pepper sauce. Mix well and spoon into the baking dish. Top with almonds. Bake at 350° for 15 to 20 minutes or until hot. Garnish with parsley. Serve with crackers.

*Fresh salmon is best. Steam one nice size salmon steak until flaky and remove skin and bones

Yield: 8-10 servings.

SPICY MARINATED SHRIMP

½ cup olive oil
½ cup red wine vinegar
2 tablespoons soy sauce
6 medium garlic cloves, minced
½ cup green onion, chopped
1 jalapeño, seeded and chopped
1 poblano pepper, seeded and
    chopped
1 red bell pepper, chopped
1 green bell pepper, chopped
    juice and zest of 2 limes
¼ cup cilantro, chopped
1 tomato, peeled, seeded
    and chopped
    salt and pepper to taste
1 pound cooked shrimp, peeled
    and deveined

Combine all ingredients, except shrimp. Blend well. Add shrimp and marinate at least four to six hours, stirring occasionally.

Yield: 6-8 servings

CHEESY CRAB CANAPÉS

1 cup processed cheese spread
1 pound crab meat, fresh or canned
¼ cup butter, softened
1 tablespoon mayonnaise
½ teaspoon seasoned salt
¼ teaspoon garlic salt
10 English muffins, halved

Translated on page 241

Combine first six ingredients and blend well. Spread generously on each muffin half. Cut each muffin half into quarters. Place on baking sheets and broil five minutes. May be frozen before broiling.

Yield: 40 servings

CRAB MOUSSE

1	(10 ½-ounce) can cream of mushroom soup
1	envelope unflavored gelatin
3	tablespoons cold water
¾	cup mayonnaise
1	(8-ounce) package cream cheese, softened
1	(6 ½-ounce) can crab meat, drained
1	small onion, finely chopped
1	cup celery, finely chopped
1	teaspoon lemon juice
1	small red pepper, finely chopped
1	small green pepper, finely chopped
	parsley for garnish

Heat soup. Dissolve gelatin in water. When dissolved, add remaining ingredients along with gelatin to soup. Mix well. Spoon into an oiled mold and chill until firm. Turn out onto a serving plate and garnish with parsley. Serve with crackers.

Yield: 8 servings

MARIANN'S PICKLED SHRIMP

6	pounds cooked shrimp, peeled
4	large onions, cut into rings
1 ½	cups salad oil
½	cup white vinegar
¼	cup prepared mustard
4	teaspoons paprika
4	teaspoons celery seed
2	(4-ounce) jars capers

Place the shrimp and onion rings in a large bowl. Mix remaining ingredients in another bowl, except for one jar of capers. Add to shrimp and onions. Marinate overnight, mixing occasionally. Just before serving, add remaining jar of capers. Can be made two to three days before serving.

Yield: 10-12 servings

ALASKAN HOT POT

1   (8-ounce) package cream cheese, softened
¼   cup mayonnaise
2   tablespoons white wine
2   (6 ½-ounce) cans crab meat, drained and flaked
1   clove fresh garlic, minced
½   teaspoon dry mustard
¼   teaspoon salt
½   teaspoon chives, chopped
1   teaspoon Worcestershire sauce
4-5   dashes of hot pepper sauce

Combine cream cheese, mayonnaise and white wine in a sauce pan on low heat until smooth. Add remaining ingredients and heat until warm without boiling. Serve warm with carrots, celery, croissants, crackers or French bread.

Yield: 8 servings

HOT CLAM DIP

2   cans clams, chopped or minced, (reserve juice of one can)
1   stick margarine, melted
1   sleeve round buttery crackers, crushed
1   medium onion, finely chopped
¼   teaspoon dill weed
    salt and pepper to taste

Mix all ingredients well and pour into a covered dish. Bake at 350° for 30 minutes. Serve hot on crackers.

Yield: 8 servings

SOUTH TEXAS SHRIMP DIP

1   cup cooked shrimp, chopped
1   (8-ounce) package cream cheese, softened
¼   cup green onion (white and green parts), chopped
¼   cup jalapeño stuffed olives (or plain olives and pickled jalapeños)
¼   cup light mayonnaise or ranch dressing
¼   teaspoon season salt
¼   teaspoon black pepper

Translated on page 242

Combine all ingredients and blend well. Garnish with more chopped olives. Serve with crackers or fresh raw vegetables.

Yield: 6-8 servings

SHRIMP SPREAD

1   (8-ounce) package cream cheese, softened
6   tablespoons catsup
2   tablespoons dry minced onion
1   tablespoon Worcestershire sauce
2   tablespoons mayonnaise
2   tablespoons butter or margarine, melted
1   small package cooked frozen shrimp, chopped

Mix all ingredients, except shrimp, blending well. Add shrimp and stir. Refrigerate overnight. Serve with crackers.

Yield: 8 servings

CRAB & CHEESE DIP

½   pound fresh crab meat
2   cups mayonnaise
2   cups Cheddar cheese, shredded
1   cup green onion, chopped
2   tablespoons horseradish
1   teaspoon lemon juice
1   teaspoon Worcestershire sauce

Combine all ingredients together and mix well. Pour into a 9-inch pie plate. Bake uncovered at 350° for 25 to 30 minutes or until hot and bubbly.

Yield: 6-8 servings

Harris Hawk

F.P.BENNETT©'95

EMPANADAS

2	cups flour
1	(6-ounce) package cream cheese, softened
2	sticks butter, softened
⅓	cup raisins
⅔	cup onion, finely chopped
3	tablespoons vegetable oil
1	pound raw chicken or raw ground beef, finely diced
3	tablespoons pine nuts or almonds, toasted
3	tablespoons pimiento-stuffed green olives, chopped
1 ¼	teaspoons salt
¾	teaspoon ground cumin
½	teaspoon crushed red pepper
	pinch of cinnamon
1	egg, beaten

In a food processor, combine flour, cream cheese and butter. Process until mixture forms a ball. Wrap in plastic and chill at least one hour or as long as three days. In a small saucepan filled with boiling water, cook raisins until softened (about five minutes). Drain and set aside. In a large skillet over medium heat, cook onion until softened but not browned, about five to seven minutes. Stir in meat, pine nuts, olives, salt, cumin, red pepper, cinnamon and raisins. Cook, stirring often, until meat is cooked thoroughly and no longer pink. Remove from heat and let cool. Preheat oven to 350°. Roll out dough about ⅛ inch thick and cut into 3-inch circles. Divide filling among pastry rounds, using about 2 teaspoons each, and brush edges with water. Fold rounds in half, forming crescents, and crimp edges with a fork. Arrange empanadas on a greased baking sheet and brush with beaten egg. Bake until golden brown, about 30 minutes.

Yield: 36 servings

ESCARGOTS IN PASTA SHELLS

24	escargots
4	tablespoons butter
4	garlic cloves, minced
24	large sea-shell shaped macaroni
2	sticks butter, softened
2	shallots, chopped
¼	cup parsley, chopped
2	teaspoons Pernod
¼	cup dry white wine
1	cup almonds, ground
½	teaspoon salt
¼	teaspoon pepper

In a large frying pan over low heat, cook escargots in butter with garlic until heated through, about four minutes. In a large pot of boiling salted water, cook pasta shells until tender, about ten minutes. Drain and arrange on a large baking sheet. In a food processor, combine butter, shallots, parsley, Pernod, wine, almonds, salt and pepper. Spoon one teaspoon of mixture into each shell. Place one escargot in each shell. Bake at 350° until hot and bubbly.

Yield: 24 servings

STEAK TARTARE

1	pound beef sirloin or tenderloin, trimmed of all fat
½	cup onion or shallots, finely minced
1	tablespoon extra virgin olive oil
1 ½	teaspoons salt
1	teaspoon freshly ground pepper
1	small garlic clove, minced
1	cup parsley, chopped

Using a large sharp knife or a food processor, mince beef. In a medium bowl, combine beef, onion, olive oil, salt, pepper and garlic. Mix gently until well blended. Form mixture into one inch balls and roll in parsley. Serve immediately with toothpicks or cover and refrigerate up to eight hours. Garnish with capers, hard cooked eggs and chopped anchovies.

Yield: 36 servings

PARTY SAUSAGE BALLS

4   pounds breakfast sausage,
        regular or hot
3   (6-ounce) cans whole mushrooms
3   (8-ounce) cans water chestnuts,
        whole or sliced
1   (16-ounce) can chunk pineapple
1   (16-ounce) jar stuffed olives
1   cup fresh parsley, chopped
        coarse black pepper

Sauce:
¼   cup light soy sauce
¼   cup sherry
1   tablespoon sugar
1 ½ teaspoons ginger
½   teaspoon garlic powder

Make sausage into one-inch balls.
Place on a cookie sheet and bake at
500° about 15 minutes until slightly
brown. Spoon into colander and drain
well. Mix together sauce ingredients
and pour over meatballs. Toss gently
to blend. (Can be frozen at this point).
At party time, stir in mushrooms,
water chestnuts, pineapple, and olives
and bake at 350° until sizzling. Turn
into a large chafing dish and sprinkle
with parsley and pepper. (Can also
add miniature cocktail sausages to this
dish.)

Yield: 40 servings

ANTIPASTO

1   (14-ounce) can marinated
        artichoke hearts, drained and
        chopped
1   (8-ounce) can sliced mushrooms,
        drained and chopped
1   (4-ounce) jar pimientos, drained
        and diced
1   cup pimiento-stuffed olives,
        drained
½   cup bell pepper, chopped
½   cup celery, chopped
½   cup vegetable oil
½   cup onions, finely chopped
3   garlic cloves, minced
½   cup vinegar
2 ½ teaspoons Italian seasoning
1   teaspoon pepper, freshly ground

Combine first six ingredients in a large
bowl and set aside. Heat oil in
saucepan over medium heat. Add
onion and garlic and cook three minutes. Add vinegar and remaining
ingredients and bring to a boil. Pour
over vegetables. Cover and refrigerate
overnight. Serve on fresh endive
leaves or with crackers and corn tortilla chips.

Yield: 5 cups

SUNDAY BRUNCH BLOODY MARYS

1	(46-ounce) can tomato juice
1 ¾	cups vodka
2	tablespoons lemon juice
1	tablespoon Worcestershire sauce
½	teaspoon salt
	few drops red pepper sauce
	margarita salt (optional)
	celery stalks (optional)

In a large pitcher combine first six ingredients. Cover and refrigerate several hours or overnight. To serve, pour into salt rimmed glasses. Use celery stalks to stir.

Yield: 16 (4 oz.) servings

SWEET STRAWBERRY DAIQUIRI

3	ounces lime juice
1	ounce grenadine
1	tablespoon sugar
9	ounces dark rum
6	strawberries crushed
	several sliced strawberries for garnish
	ice

Sweeten lime juice with grenadine and sugar. Combine rum and strawberries. Place in blender with crushed ice and blend.

Yield: 4 servings

MI CHILADA (MY CHILLED ONE)

	margarita salt
	fresh lime, squeezed
	ice
	beer

Salt rim of a pilsner glass. Squeeze juice from one lime into glass. Fill with ice. Pour beer over lime and ice mixture and stir.

In some parts of Mexico this is served as a chaser for tequila shots.

MONT BLANC

1	ounce Chambord Liqueur (raspberry)
1	ounce vodka
1	ounce half and half or cream
1	large scoop vanilla ice cream

Mix ingredients in a blender for 20 seconds. Serve.

Yield: 4 servings

VELVET HAMMER

12	scoops ice milk
2	ounces Cointreau or Triple Sec
2	ounces White Crema de Cocoa

Place ingredients in blender and mix. Pour into compotes and place in freezer. Great for simple dessert or after dinner drink.

Yield: 4 servings

SASSY SANGRIA

	ice cubes
1	(6-ounce) can lemonade, thawed
12	ounces club soda or seltzer water
½	cup superfine sugar
1	bottle red, white or rosé wine
1	shot of brandy (optional)
	slices of apple, oranges, lemons
6-12	small grape bunches

Fill two quart pitcher with ice. Add lemonade and mix well. Add club soda, sugar, wine, brandy, apples, oranges and lemons. Blend well. Garnish with bunches of grapes draping over the side of the pitcher.

Yield: 8 servings

JUDY'S SPICED TEA

8 cups water
6 cinnamon stick tea bags
3 whole cloves
4 cups Hawaiian punch
2 cups apple cider
1 cup sugar

In a 3-quart saucepan, steep tea bags in water. Add cloves. In a separate container mix punch and cider. When tea has brewed, remove tea bags and cloves. Add sugar until completely dissolved. Pour punch mixture into tea and blend. This can be served hot or cold.

Yield: 1 gallon

WASSAIL

2 quarts apple cider
2 cups orange juice
1 cup lemon juice
5 cups pineapple juice
5 sticks of cinnamon
1 teaspoon whole cloves
1 cup honey
1 large orange, sliced for garnish

Simmer all ingredients, except orange slices. Do not boil. Simmer one hour or longer. Strain. Serve hot. Garnish with orange slices.

HOT SPICED PINEAPPLE

1 (46-ounce) can pineapple juice
1 cup apple juice
½ cup packed light brown sugar
¼ cup butter or margarine
1 teaspoon ground cinnamon
¼ teaspoon ground nutmeg
⅛ teaspoon ground cloves
1 cup light rum
maraschino cherries, for garnish
pineapple chunks, for garnish
lime slices, for garnish

Combine juices, sugar, butter and spices in a large saucepan. Simmer over medium to low heat for 15 minutes. Pour in rum. Ladle into glasses. Garnish with fruit.

Yield: 9 servings

SPARKLING PUNCH

1	(12-ounce) can frozen lemonade
1	(12-ounce) can frozen orange juice
1	(46-ounce) can pineapple juice
3	cups sugar
5	bananas, pureed
6	cups water
2	quarts ginger ale

Combine all ingredients, except for ginger ale. Can be frozen in gallon containers. Pour into punch bowl. Add ginger ale just before serving.

Yield: 1 ½ gallons

CHAMPAGNE PUNCH BOWL

1	cup fresh or frozen strawberries, hulled
1	cup fresh or frozen peach slices
⅓	cup sugar
3	bottles chilled champagne
	strawberries, hulled
	crushed ice

Puree strawberries and peaches. Mix in sugar. Refrigerate mixture for 30 minutes. Spoon into bottom of punch bowl. Add champagne to punch bowl. Arrange remaining berries and ice in punch bowl.

Yield: 3 quarts

PUNCH FOR A BUNCH

2	(6-ounce) packages peach or apricot flavored gelatin
1	cup boiling water
3	cups warm water
1	(12-ounce) can frozen lemonade
1	(46-ounce) can peach or apricot nectar
1	(46-ounce) can pineapple juice
½	gallon cold water
4	quarts ginger ale, chilled

Dissolve gelatin in boiling water. Add warm water, lemonade, nectar, and pineapple juice. Stir well. Add ½ gallon water. Freeze in four equal size containers. Remove from freezer 20 to 30 minutes before serving to allow punch to thaw to a slushy consistency. Add ginger ale just before serving.

Yield: 40 servings

CHRISTMAS EGGNOG PUNCH

12	eggs	Beat eggs and sugar until lemon-col-
¾	cup sugar	ored. Stir in water, orange juice and
10	cups water	lemon juice. Place scoops of ice cream
1	(48-ounce) can frozen orange	in punch bowl. Pour mixture over ice
	juice, thawed	cream. Add ginger ale just before
1	cup lemon juice	serving.
½	gallon vanilla ice cream	Yield: 32 servings
2	quarts ginger ale	

HOT CHOCOLATE

1	(1-pound) box chocolate	Mix all ingredients together. For each
	powdered milk mix	cup of hot cocoa use ⅓ cup mix to one
1	(1-pound) box powdered sugar	cup hot water.
1	(8-quart) box instant powdered	*This makes a great hostess gift when*
	milk	*placed in a decorative jar!*
1	(11-ounce) jar powdered non-	
	dairy creamer	

In the early 1900's, as Harlingen's founder pursued his vision of a canal-covered agricultural oasis in South Texas, he discussed his engineering plans with Col. Uriah Lott, the president of the railroad being built through the area. Col. Lott was of Dutch descent, and his grandmother was born Eliza Van Harlingen in the town in Holland named for her family. In honor of Col. Lott, Lon C. Hill changed the name of his town to Harlingen. Harlingen was officially chartered on April 15, 1910.

Soups & Salads

OYSTERS ROCKEFELLER SOUP

5	tablespoons butter	
5	tablespoons flour	
2	garlic cloves, minced	
1	bunch green onions, chopped	
2 ½	cups oysters, drained and minced	
1 ½	cups chicken stock	
3	cups cream, scalded	
1	(20-ounce) package frozen spinach, cooked and drained	
	salt, cayenne pepper, hot red pepper sauce, and nutmeg to taste	

Melt butter and stir in flour. Add garlic and onions and cook over medium high heat until onions are transparent. Add oysters and cook until oysters are firm. Add chicken stock and cream; stir well to combine. Add spinach and bring to a boil. Remove soup from heat and allow to cook. Process in a blender or food processor until well blended. Season with salt and other spices.

Yield: 6 servings

SWEET POTATO CORN CHOWDER

6	slices bacon
3	tablespoons yellow onion, chopped
½	cup celery, chopped
3	tablespoons green pepper, chopped
1	cup sweet potato, cubed
2	cups water
½	teaspoon salt
½	teaspoon thyme
1	bay leaf
3	tablespoons flour
½	cup milk
1 ½	cups hot milk
2	cups frozen corn
2	tablespoons parsley, chopped
½	teaspoon honey

Dice bacon and cook in a large soup pot until crisp. Remove bacon and sauté onion, celery and green pepper in remaining bacon fat. Add sweet potato, water, salt, thyme and bay leaf. Simmer for 20 minutes or until the sweet potato is tender. Mix the flour and ½ cup milk to make a smooth paste. Slowly stir paste into soup and cook an additional ten minutes. Add hot milk, corn, parsley and honey. Simmer until heated thoroughly. Ladle into bowls and garnish with bacon pieces.

Yield: 5-6 servings

SOUTHWESTERN CURRIED BUTTERNUT SQUASH SOUP

4	tablespoons butter
2	cups yellow onions, finely chopped
4-5	teaspoons curry powder
2	medium size butternut squash
2	apples, peeled, cored and chopped
3	cups chicken stock
1	cup apple juice
	salt and freshly ground black pepper, to taste
1	cup whipping cream
1	serrano pepper, finely minced
	fresh lime juice to taste
	fresh cilantro

Melt butter in a large soup pot. Add chopped onions and curry powder and cook, covered, over low heat until onions are tender. Meanwhile, peel squash (a regular vegetable peeler works best), scrape out the seeds, and chop flesh. When onions are tender, pour in chicken stock. Add squash and apples, and cook about 25 minutes or until apples are tender. Pour soup in batches into a blender or food processor and puree until smooth. Return to pot and add apple juice. Season to taste with salt and pepper. Simmer gently to heat through. Before serving, add one cup whipping cream, serrano pepper and lime juice, to taste. Garnish each bowl with fresh chopped cilantro.

While visiting the southern tip of Texas in the late 1890's businessman Lon C. Hill began to dream of a desert land made fertile by the construction of canals and water systems. Hill helped pursuade his friend B.F. Yoakum of the Missouri Pacific Railroad to lay tracks from Corpus Christi to Brownsville, with a branch traversing what would someday be known as "the Valley." At the junction was a tiny trading post catering to the surrounding ranches, where Lon C. Hill had built his home. According to pioneer peace officer and early historian Gus T. Jones, the community was known early on as Six-Shooter Junction...due to the fact that its first Anglo-Saxon population consisted mostly of Texas Rangers, Border Patrolmen and Lon C. Hill.

SLOW COOK FRENCH ONION SOUP

3-4 large onions, sliced in rings
½ stick butter
7 bouillon cubes
1 cup water
1 ½ cups dry white wine
½ cup cooking sherry
2 slices French bread, sliced
and toasted
Swiss cheese slices

Melt butter in large, non-stick fry pan. Add onions, and slow cook over very low heat, turning occasionally, until very soft (approximately two hours). In a large sauce pan, dissolve bouillon cubes in water, wine and sherry. Bring to a boil and add onions and butter mixture. Let simmer, covered, for approximately two hours. Stir occasionally and add extra wine if necessary. Ladle soup into two oven proof crocks and top with french bread swiss cheese slices. Place in broiler for several minutes until cheese melts and bubbles.

For cheese lovers, add an extra layer of cheese and broil again! Secret to success is slow, long cooking and lots of wine!

Yield: 4 servings

Turn-of-the-century railroad workers christened the small town site that would someday be Harlingen as "Rattlesnake Junction" because it seemed there were more rattlesnakes, fleas, and scorpions in the desert area than there ever would be humans. By 1991, Harlingen had grown to a community of...blessed with a stable government, a strong volunteer ethic, and an abundance of civic pride...and would be named an "All America City."

FALL HARVEST SOUP

4 tablespoons butter
6 carrots, peeled and sliced
2 medium all-purpose potatoes,
   peeled and sliced
1 onion, chopped
1 cup chicken broth
½ teaspoon salt
½ teaspoon black pepper
⅛ teaspoon garlic powder
⅛ teaspoon dried thyme
1 cup half and half
  ground nutmeg
  sweet paprika
  parsley, finely minced

Melt butter in a saucepan. Add vegetables and cook over low heat approximately 15 minutes, stirring occasionally. Add broth, salt, pepper, garlic and thyme. Cover and cook slowly 45 minutes. Pour into a blender or food processor and puree. Return to saucepan and reheat over low heat. Stir in half and half, a pinch of nutmeg and a pinch of paprika. To serve, sprinkle each serving with minced parsley and additional nutmeg. If too thick, thin with a little milk to get the desired texture.

Soup can be prepared ahead at two separate points. It can be made one or two days ahead after pureeing and finished prior to serving. The soup can also be made in its entirety ahead hours before serving and slowly reheat and garnished prior to serving.

Yield: 4-6 servings

BROCCOLI CHEESE SOUP

4	cups water
4	cubes chicken bouillon
1	cup celery, chopped
1	cup onion, chopped
2	tablespoons butter or margarine
1	pound processed cheese, cubed
2 ½	cups potatoes, diced
1	cup carrots, diced
1	(10-ounce) box frozen broccoli
2	(10 ½-ounce) cans cream of chicken soup

In large saucepan, simmer together water and bouillon for 20 minutes. Sauté celery and onion in butter until tender. Add to bouillon. Add potatoes, carrots, frozen broccoli and cream of chicken soup. Cook for about an hour or until carrots are tender. Add cheese and heat only until it melts. For a heartier soup, add two to three chicken breasts, cooked and diced.

RIO GRANDE CASSOULET

1	tablespoon margarine
1	cup onion, chopped
1	garlic clove, minced
2	(16-ounce) cans of Great Northern Beans (or Navy Beans)
4	cups chicken, cooked and cubed
3	cups chicken broth
2	teaspoons ground cumin
2	teaspoons oregano
1	(4-ounce) can chopped green chilis
	dash of cayenne pepper

Sauté onion and garlic in margarine until vegetables are translucent. Add remaining ingredients and let simmer 25 to 30 minutes. Serve with chopped tomatoes, sour cream, tortilla chips and shredded Monterey Jack cheese.

CORN SOUP SOUTHWEST

4	cups fresh corn kernels (or canned corn, drained)
1	red bell pepper, chopped
¼	cup onion, chopped
2	tablespoons butter
2	tablespoons flour
	salt and pepper to taste
2	cups chicken broth
2	cups milk
1	cup Cheddar cheese, shredded
1	(4-ounce) can green chilis, chopped
1	cup bacon, cooked and crumbled
	tortilla chips

Sauté red pepper, onion and corn in butter until tender. Add flour, salt and pepper, cooking for one minute. Gradually add broth, alternating with milk until thickened. Add cheddar cheese, ½ cup bacon and green chilis. Be careful not to overheat. Serve in individual bowls. Add four to five tortilla chips per bowl and garnish with remaining bacon.

Translated on page 236

CREOLE SHRIMP SOUP

½	cup margarine, butter or cooking oil
¼	cup flour
1	cup onion, chopped
½	cup celery, chopped
1	garlic clove, minced
2	cans low sodium chicken broth
1	(28-ounce) can tomatoes, diced and undrained
½	cup white wine
2	tablespoons parsley, chopped
1	tablespoon lemon juice
1	bay leaf
½	teaspoon salt
¼	teaspoon cayenne pepper
¼	teaspoon saffron (optional-- but really adds)
1 ½	pounds raw shrimp, peeled and de-veined

In large soup pot, melt margarine over medium heat. To prepare roux, slowly blend in flour and stir constantly until mixture is smooth and a light brown color. Add onion, celery, and garlic and continue stirring until vegetables are tender. Gradually stir in chicken broth. Add remaining ingredients except shrimp. Bring to a boil, then simmer for ten minutes. Add shrimp and cook for five minutes more or until seafood is pink.

Yield: 6 servings

Translated on page 235

WEEZIE'S VICHYSQUASH SOUP

1	medium onion, chopped
2	tablespoons butter
1	(14-ounce) can chicken broth
1 ½	pounds yellow squash, sliced
1	cup light cream
	salt and pepper

Sauté onion in butter. Add broth and squash and cook until tender. Cool. In a food processor, blend until smooth. Blend in cream and season to taste. Serve in small wine glasses before dinner.

Yield: 5 cups

VICHYSSOISE

7	leeks, white part only, sliced
4	tablespoons butter
6	white potatoes, peeled and thinly sliced
2	teaspoons salt
5	cups low sodium chicken broth
2	cups half and half
	pinch of nutmeg
½	teaspoon white pepper
1	cup heavy cream

Sauté leeks in butter eight to ten minutes. Add potatoes, salt and broth. Simmer 30 minutes or until potatoes are very tender. Puree potato mixture in food processor. Add half and half, nutmeg and pepper. Chill well. When ready to serve, stir in heavy cream.

Yield: 6-8 servings.

LONGHORN CATTLE COMPANY BEAN SOUP

1	pound pinto beans
½	pound chopped smoked brisket
1 or 2	large yellow onions, chopped
	garlic salt and pepper to taste

Combine ingredients in a dutch oven. Cook three to four hours on low heat, stirring occasionally.

Bill and Lisa Turner - *The Longhorn Cattle Company in San Benito is an excellent place for down home barbecue and their beans are famous all over the Rio Grande Valley.*

BLACK BEAN AND CORN CHILI

¼ cup onion, chopped
2 cloves garlic, minced
1 (15-ounce) can black beans, drained and rinsed or 2 cups fresh black beans, drained
1 cup canned chopped tomatoes with juice
1 cup frozen corn, thawed
1 teaspoon tomato paste
1 tablespoon chili powder
1 teaspoon ground cumin
½ cup green bell pepper, chopped

Spray skillet with vegetable spray. Sauté onion, garlic and bell pepper until tender. Add drained black beans, tomatoes with juice and corn. Simmer for about 15 minutes. Add chili powder, cumin and tomato paste. Simmer for another ten minutes. Serve warm.

Yield: 4 servings

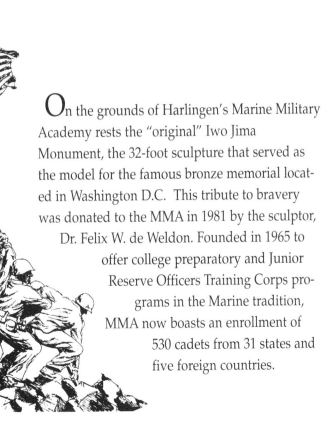

On the grounds of Harlingen's Marine Military Academy rests the "original" Iwo Jima Monument, the 32-foot sculpture that served as the model for the famous bronze memorial located in Washington D.C. This tribute to bravery was donated to the MMA in 1981 by the sculptor, Dr. Felix W. de Weldon. Founded in 1965 to offer college preparatory and Junior Reserve Officers Training Corps programs in the Marine tradition, MMA now boasts an enrollment of 530 cadets from 31 states and five foreign countries.

CREAMY SHRIMP SALAD

1   pound medium cooked shrimp, peeled and deveined
2   hard cooked eggs, chopped
1   cup celery, chopped
½   cup onion, chopped
2   tablespoons sweet pickle relish
⅓   cup mayonnaise
⅓   cup sour cream
1   tablespoon catsup
2   dashes hot pepper sauce (Optional)
1   teaspoon Worcestershire sauce
lettuce leaves

Combine all ingredients except lettuce and mix well. Refrigerate for at least two hours before serving. Serve on lettuce leaves.

Yield: 4 servings

CONGEALED SHRIMP SALAD

2   (3-ounce) packages cream cheese, softened
1   (10 ½-ounce) can tomato soup
⅓   cup bell pepper, chopped
½   cup onion, finely chopped
½   cup celery, finely chopped
2   tablespoons unflavored gelatin, dissolved in ½ cup water
1   cup mayonnaise
2   pounds cooked shrimp, peeled and chopped

Melt cream cheese in tomato soup. Add remaining ingredients, adding mayonnaise and shrimp last. Oil mold with non-stick cooking spray and wipe out lightly. Rinse with water and pour shrimp mixture into mold. Refrigerate until firm.

Yield: 6 servings

GREEN SALAD WITH PEPPERCORN DRESSING

1	head Boston lettuce
1	head Romaine lettuce
1	head Bibb lettuce
1	can artichoke bottoms, cut into bite-size pieces
½	can hearts of palm, sliced thickly
½	pound fresh mushrooms, sliced
5-6	cherry tomatoes, halved
½	purple onion, sliced and separated into rings
1	(4-ounce) can sliced black olives

Peppercorn Dressing:

¾	cup sour cream
½	cup mayonnaise
2	tablespoons fresh lemon juice
1	teaspoon Worcestershire sauce
3-4	teaspoons black pepper, coarsley ground
1	cube beef bouillon, dissolved in 4 teaspoons hot water

Wash and dry lettuce leaves and tear into bite sized pieces. Chill well along with other vegetables.

To make dressing, combine all ingredients and whisk until well-blended. Refrigerate in a tightly covered container for at least three hours. (Will keep in refrigerator for at least ten days).

To serve, mix all vegetables together and toss with Peppercorn dressing.

JICAMA SALAD

1	medium red onion, thinly sliced lightly salted water
1	head red leaf lettuce
2	pounds jicama, peeled and julienned

Vinaigrette:

3	tablespoons fresh lemon juice
1 ½	tablespoons fresh lime juice
¼	teaspoon lemon peel, shredded
¼	teaspoon salt
¾	cup olive oil
6	tablespoons peanut oil

Soak red onion in lightly salted water for two hours. To make vinaigrette, blend citrus juices, lemon peel and salt in a small bowl. Whisk in olive oil in slow stream. Repeat with peanut oil. To serve, arrange lettuce on platter. Drain onion well, pat dry and transfer to a large bowl. Add jicama and vinaigrette and toss. Place jicama and onion on platter with lettuce and serve.

Yield: 8 servings

WINTER SPINACH SALAD

1	pound spinach, washed, dried and torn into bite-size pieces
1	red onion, sliced thinly
8	slices bacon, cooked and crumbled
	dash of pepper
4	hard cooked eggs, chopped
1	can water chestnuts, sliced
¼	pound mushrooms, sliced (optional)
½	cup Swiss cheese, shredded (optional)

Dressing:

1	cup oil
⅓	cup cider vinegar
½	cup sugar
1	teaspoon dry minced onion
½	teaspoon paprika
½	teaspoon dry mustard

Chill all salad ingredients well. To make dressing, whisk together all ingredients until well blended. To serve, mix together salad ingredients and toss with dressing.

Yield: 8-10 servings

Translated on page 239

Ferruginous Pygmy Owl

F.P.Bennett

REFRIGERATOR SLAW

1   (3-pound) head cabbage,
    chopped
1   large onion, sliced
1   cup plus 2 teaspoons sugar
¾   cup vegetable oil
1   level teaspoon salt
1   teaspoon celery seed
1   teaspoon dry mustard
1   cup white vinegar

Two or more days before serving, layer cabbage and onion in large bowl. Sprinkle one cup sugar over vegetables but do not mix. In a medium sauce pan, combine rest of ingredients including the two teaspoons of sugar. Bring to a boil and cook for three minutes. Pour over cabbage. Cover bowl with foil and let stand at room temperature four to six hours. Do not mix, but press and pack down several times. Refrigerate slaw, covered, for at least two days before serving. To serve, toss and drain extra liquid.

Great with barbecues!

Yield: 8-10 servings

GARBANZO SPINACH SALAD

12   cups fresh spinach, torn into
     bite size pieces
½   cup olive oil
4   cups fresh mushrooms, sliced
2   tablespoons sugar
1   (15-ounce) can Garbanzo beans,
     drained
1-2 tablespoons white wine vinegar
1   cup red onion, thinly sliced and
     separated into rings
½   cup pitted black olives, chopped
     croutons, if desired

In a very large bowl, combine all salad ingredients except croutons and toss. Cover and chill well. To make dressing, combine olive oil, sugar and enough wine vinegar for desired flavor. Blend well and refrigerate. To serve, toss salad with dressing and top with croutons. Serve immediately.

Yield: 8 servings

LAYERED SPINACH SALAD

2　packages fresh spinach, washed
　　and chopped
1　pound bacon, cooked and
　　crumbled
1　(10-ounce) package frozen peas
1　bunch green onions, chopped
8　hard cooked eggs, sliced
1　box mushrooms, sliced
1　cup Swiss cheese, shredded

Dressing:

1　cup mayonnaise
½　pint sour cream
2　tablespoons wine vinegar
　　dash salt
　　dash pepper
　　dash dry mustard

In a 9 x 13-inch dish, spread out one package spinach. Place bacon on top of spinach, followed by peas and onions. Layer the eggs and follow with the other package of spinach. Place sliced mushrooms on spinach and frost with the dressing. Sprinkle a layer of Swiss cheese on top. Keep refrigerated until time to serve.

This salad gets better with each day.

Yield: 10 servings

CORNBREAD SALAD

2　packages jalapeño cornbread mix
1　bunch green onions, chopped
1　green bell pepper, chopped
2　tomatoes, chopped
1　(16-ounce) can corn, drained
1　cup Cheddar cheese, shredded
8　slices bacon, cooked and
　　crumbled
1 ½　cups mayonnaise
½　cup sour cream
½　teaspoon chili powder
　　pepper to taste
　　avocado slices to garnish

Translated on page 237

Prepare cornbread using package directions. Cool and crumble into bowl. Add vegetables, cheese, bacon, mayonnaise, sour cream and seasonings. Mix well and chill overnight. Garnish with avocado slices.

Yield: 10 servings

ORANGE ALMOND CHICKEN SALAD

4-6	bonelesss, skinless chicken breasts
	mesquite marinade
1	head Romaine lettuce, torn
1	small can mandarin oranges
⅓	cup slivered almonds, toasted
1	cup celery, chopped (optional)
1	tablespoon green onions, chopped (optional)

Dressing:

¼	cup corn oil (not olive oil)
2	tablespoons sugar
2	tablespoons tarragon vinegar
¼	teaspoon salt
⅛	teaspoon almond flavoring

Marinate chicken breasts overnight in refrigerator. Grill chicken breasts until desired doneness and slice into thin strips when cooled. To make dressing, combine oil, sugar, vinegar, salt, and almond flavoring in a jar. Shake vigorously and chill at least one hour. To serve, combine greens, chicken breasts, and oranges in a large bowl and sprinkle with almonds. Pour dressing over salad and toss gently to coat.

Yield: 4-6 servings

BOW TIE PASTA CHICKEN SALAD

4	large bone-in chicken breasts
1	(16-ounce) box bow tie pasta, cooked "al dente"
1	bunch green onions, chopped
1	(8-ounce) can sliced black olives
½	cup mayonnaise
½	teaspoon curry powder
½	teaspoon lemon juice
	salt and pepper to taste

Boil chicken breasts in a large pot. Season and cook for 30 minutes. Let cool and pull chicken from bone into bite size pieces. Combine chicken, pasta, black olives and green onions. Mix together mayonnaise, curry powder and lemon juice and pour over chicken and pasta mixture. Toss gently to coat. Salt and pepper to taste.

This dish is great for a crowd!! Serve with fresh fruit and hot french bread.

Yield: 6-8 servings

FIESTA AVOCADO SALAD

2   large avocados, chopped in
      large chunks
1   stalk celery, chopped
⅓   cup red bell pepper, chopped
¼   cup green olives, sliced
1   fresh jalapeño, chopped
¼   cup fresh cilantro, chopped
      juice of 2-3 fresh limes

Mix all ingredients together. Serve on lettuce leaves with a main course.

This salad is a beautiful addition to chalupas or fajitas! For a stronger flavor, add onions.

Yield: 4 servings

CHICKEN AND AVOCADO SALAD WITH BACON DRESSING

2   cans chicken broth
6   boneless, skinless, chicken
      breast halves
2   avocados, cubed
2   tablespoons lemon juice
½   cup green onions, chopped
Dressing:
½   pound bacon
1   large egg, at room temperature
5   teaspoons fresh lemon juice
1   teaspoon Dijon mustard
¼   teaspoon salt
¼   teaspoon white pepper
½   cup vegetable oil

Translated on page 238

Toss avacados with lemon juice and set aside. In skillet, bring chicken broth to a boil and add chicken breasts. Reduce heat and simmer, turning once until breasts are done. Remove skillet from heat and let chicken cool in broth for 30 minutes.

To make dressing, cook bacon until crisp and drain, reserving ¼ cup bacon drippings. Allow to cool for 15 minutes. In food processor or blender, combine egg, lemon juice, mustard, salt and white pepper. With motor running, add reserved bacon fat and vegetable oil in a stream. Add bacon and process for five seconds. To serve, cut chicken into cubes. Combine with avocado and green onion. Pour dressing over chicken mixture and toss gently. Serve immediately.

Yield: 4-6 servings

JUDY'S CHICKEN PASTA SALAD

3	tablespoons red wine vinegar
1	tablespoon fresh or dried basil, chopped
1	garlic clove, minced
1	teaspoon salt
¼	teaspoon pepper
2	(6-ounce) cans chicken, chopped
1	(10-ounce) package garden rotini pasta
1	cup mayonnaise
1	cup cherry tomatoes, quartered
¼	cup red onion, thinly sliced
½	cup sliced black olives

Combine vinegar, basil, garlic, salt, pepper and chicken. Cook pasta according to package directions. Rinse in cold water and add to chicken mixture. Add remaining ingredients and mix well. Chill until ready to serve.

Yield: 4-6 servings

SUPER SHELL PASTA SALAD

2 ¾	cups uncooked shell macaroni
1	cup cherry tomatoes, halved
1	cup Cheddar cheese, shredded
½	cup green onions, chopped
½	cup ripe olive, pitted and sliced
1	medium size green pepper, chopped
¼	cup vegetable oil
2	tablespoons lemon juice
2	tablespoons white wine vinegar
1	teaspoon dried whole dill weed
1	teaspoon dried whole oregano
½	teaspoon salt
⅛	teaspoon pepper

Cook macaroni according to package directions. Drain, rinse with cold water and drain again. Combine macaroni, tomatoes, cheese, green onions, olives and green pepper and set aside. To make dressing, combine oil and remaining ingredients. Pour over macaroni mixture and toss gently. Cover and chill several hours.

The longer it marinates, the better the salad!

Yield: 8 servings

SALADE DE POMME DE TERRE ET HARICOTS VERT

2   pounds red potatoes
1   pound haricots vert (green beans)
5   tablespoons mustard vinaigrette
¼   cup feta cheese, crumbled
    salt and pepper to taste

Preheat oven to 450°. Clean and quarter potatoes and place in a roasting pan. Coat with two tablespoons of mustard vinaigrette and roast potatoes for approximately 30 minutes until soft. Boil green beans in water for two minutes. Rinse with cold water to stop them from over cooking. Toss beans with three tablespoons of vinaigrette and place in a serving bowl. Mound potatoes over beans and top with feta cheese. Serve cold or at room temperature.

Yield: 6 servings

Ringed Kingfisher
in Cypress

ARTICHOKE-RICE SALAD

1   (6-ounce) package long grain
    and wild rice mix
1   (14-ounce) can artichoke hearts,
    drained and chopped
1   (2-ounce) jar pimiento, drained
    and chopped
3   green onions with tops, chopped
1   cup celery, chopped
1   teaspoon curry powder
    tomato wedges for garnish

Cook rice according to package directions, omitting butter. Add remaining ingredients except tomatoes and mix well. Cover and chill for at least one hour. Garnish with tomato wedges.

Yield: 8 servings

WATERCRESS-BLUE CHEESE SALAD

1   large bunch watercress, rinsed
    and stems removed
4   green onions, chopped
3   tablespoons Garlic French
    Vinaigrette (see page 58)
¼   cup sliced almonds, toasted
½   cup blue cheese, crumbled

Toss watercress and onions together. Pour on dressing and toss very lightly. Sprinkle with almonds and blue cheese.

Yield: 4 servings

Long before Harlingen was incorporated as a city, original Spanish land grantees and their descendents had created a rich cultural, social and economic life for themselves on the ranches of South Texas. The present city limits cover what was once part of the Las Prietas, Providencia, Olmales, Muerto and Los Clamores ranches. Names of other "ranchos" in the surrounding area...La India, Paso Real, Santa Teresa, and La Cruzita for example... also speak of the rich Hispanic influence in our history and culture.

MARINATED PEA SALAD

1 (11-ounce) can shoe peg corn, drained

1 (14 ½-ounce) can french style green beans, drained

1 (15 ¼-ounce) can peas, drained

1 cup celery, chopped

1 cup red onion, chopped

1 cup green pepper, chopped

1 (2-ounce) jar pimentos, drained

½ cup oil

½ cup cider vinegar

1 cup sugar

½ teaspoon garlic salt

dash salt and pepper

dash paprika

Combine all ingredients and mix well. Refrigerate for one to two days.

This salad gets better with each day!!!!

Yield: 12 servings

MARINATED TORTELLINI WITH VEGETABLES

1 (9-ounce) package cheese filled tortellini, cooked and drained

1 red bell pepper, cut into 1-inch pieces

1 green bell pepper, cut into 1-inch pieces

½ pound small mushrooms

Dressing:

½ cup olive oil

¼ cup white wine vinegar

2 tablespoons parsley, chopped

2 garlic cloves, minced

1 teaspoon basil, dried and crushed

1 teaspoon oregano, dried

salt and pepper to taste

Combine cooked tortellini, bell peppers and mushrooms in a medium bowl and set aside. To make dressing, combine oil, vinegar, parsley, garlic, basil, oregano, salt and pepper in a small jar with a tight lid. Shake vigourously until well blended. Pour the marinade over the tortellini and vegetables and toss gently to combine. Refrigerate covered for 24 hours. Before serving, bring to room temperature.

Yield: 6 servings

PISTACHIO FLUFF

1   box dry pistachio pudding
1   (9-ounce) container cool whip
1   (20-ounce) can crushed
     pineapple
¾   cup small marshmallows

Mix ingredients thoroughly and refrigerate several hours before serving.

Yield: 6-8 servings

Translated on page 237

MANGO SALAD

3   (3-ounce) packages lemon
     gelatin
3   cups boiling water
1   (8-ounce) package cream
     cheese, softened
1   (20-ounce) can mangoes
1   cup mango juice

Dressing:
1   cup sour cream
3-4 tablespoons honey

Translated on page 236

Dissolve gelatin in boiling water. In blender, combine cream cheese, mangoes and mango juice. Stir in some of the gelatin mixture until blender is full. Blend. Pour blender mixture into bowl with remaining gelatin and stir well. Pour into an oiled mold and chill until firm. Turn onto a serving platter and drizzle dressing over salad. Garnish with mangoes and lemon wedges.

Yield: 2 (2-quart) molds

PALM COURT YUM YUM SALAD

2   small boxes orange flavored
     gelatin
2   cups boiling water
3   cups mini-marshmallows
1   (8-ounce) can crushed pineapple
½   pint whipping cream
¼   cup mayonnaise
1   cup American cheese, shredded
    Juice of one lemon

Combine first four ingredients and let thicken a bit. Add remaining ingredients and combine well. Chill until congealed and serve!

You'll go "Yum-Yum!"

Joe Baldwin - Owner of the Palm Court Restaurant, located in the heart of Brownsville, a true hot spot for lunch in the Rio Grande Valley.

GRAPEFRUIT SALAD

4   grapefruit
2   small boxes lemon gelatin
    pineapple juice
1   (4-ounce) package cream cheese,
    softened
½   cup mayonnaise
1   package unflavored gelatin
½   cup evaporated milk, chilled
½   teaspoon lemon juice

Halve grapefruit and scoop out pulp and save. Squeeze grapfruit juice into a bowl. Add enough pineapple juice to make three cups. Soften gelatin in two tablespoons water. Heat half of the grapefruit/pineapple juice and add both packages of lemon gelatin and unflavored gelatin. Stir to dissolve and add remaining grapefruit/pineapple juice. Mix well. When cool, remove one half cup of this mixture and set aside for topping. Add chilled grapefruit pulp to remaining mixture and fill grapefruit halves. Chill. To make topping, whip chilled evaporated milk and lemon juice and add softened cream cheese and mayonnaise. Beat well and combine with ½ cup juice mixture. Beat until thick. Spoon on top of grapefruit cups and chill. Can be made in glass dish instead of in grapefruit skins.

Yield: 8 servings

Parks have been a "Quality of Life" consideration from the very beginning. When Harlingen's founder Lon C. Hill, plotted the original town site he donated and dedicated three sites as parks. Completed in 1990, the 48 acre sports complex is the center of the city's recreation department that attracts teams and tournaments from throughout the Southwest. The parks system was a "key player" in the Keep America Beautiful and Keep Texas Beautiful honors awarded to the city.

MOM'S PINEAPPLE CHEESE SALAD

1	envelope unflavored gelatin
½	cup cool water
1	cup crushed pineapple
¼	cup sugar
	juice of ½ lemon
1	cup Cheddar cheese, shredded
1	cup cream, whipped

Dissolve gelatin in water. In a small saucepan, cook pineapple, sugar and lemon juice for five minutes. Pour gelatin into this mixture and place in refrigerator until set (not completely gelled). In a medium size bowl, mix together cheese and whip cream. Fold gelatin mixture into whip cream mixture. Pour in a shallow pan, spread, and chill until firm (It will be soft but can be cut into serving slices. This salad is too soft to mold.). To serve, place slices on lettuce leaf and garnish with a dollop of mayonnaise and a stuffed olive.

STRAWBERRY KIWI SALAD

2	oranges, peeled and sliced across the sections
2	cups strawberries, sliced
2	large kiwi fruit, peeled and sliced
1	small banana, peeled and sliced
1	tablespoon currants (optional)

On small platter make a bed of orange wheels. In a large bowl, combine strawberries, kiwi, and bananas. Add currants. Mix gently and mound on oranges.

Yield: 4 servings

STRAWBERRY LETTUCE SALAD

2	heads Romaine or green leaf lettuce, torn into bite size pieces
1-2	pints strawberries, cut into halves
1	medium Bermuda onion, thinly sliced

Dressing:

1	cup olive oil
⅓	cup raspberry vinegar or wine vinegar
1 ½	tablespoons sugar
¼	teaspoon pepper
	Juice of 2 lemons

Combine dressing ingredients in a glass container and mix well. Chill at least two hours. To serve, arrange lettuce, strawberries and onion in glass bowl. Shake dressing well and toss with salad.

Yield: 6-8 servings

STRAWBERRY-BANANA SALAD

1	large package strawberry-banana gelatin
2	(10-ounce) packages frozen strawberries, thawed and sliced
5-6	bananas, mashed
1	tablespoon lemon juice
1	cup pecans, chopped
1	small can crushed pineapple
1	pint sour cream

Dissolve gelatin in two cups hot water and let cool. Add strawberries, bananas, lemon juice, pecans and pineapple. Pour one half of mixture into 9 x 13- inch glass dish and chill until firm. Spread with sour cream. Pour remaining mixture on top. Chill until firm.

Yield: 12 servings

CREAMY FRUIT SALAD

1   (8-ounce) can pineapple tidbits, drained
1   (11-ounce) can mandarin oranges, drained
1   cup seedless grapes
1   cup tiny marshmallows
1   cup coconut
2   cups sour cream
¼   teaspoon salt

Mix fruit together. Blend together marshmallows, coconut, sour cream and salt and add to the fruit mixture. Chill overnight.

Yield: 8 servings

MUSTARD VINAIGRETTE DRESSING

⅓   cup Dijon mustard
1   tablespoon sugar
2   tablespoons fresh sage, chopped
1   tablespoon fresh rosemary, chopped
3   tablespoons white wine vinegar
¼   cup extra virgin olive oil
½   cup shallots, chopped

Whisk mustard, sugar, vinegar and olive oil together. Add chopped herbs and shallots. Cover and refrigerate until ready to use. Can be made three days in advance.

SOUTHWEST DRESSING

1   bunch cilantro
2   cloves garlic
1   jalapeño
¼   cup white wine vinegar
¼   cup water
½   teaspoon salt
2   cups plain, nonfat yogurt

Pureé cilantro, garlic, jalapeños, vinegar, water and salt in a food processor. Fold into yogurt and blend well.

Yield: 2 cups

MINT DIP FOR FRESH FRUIT

¾ cup sour cream, regular or
    low-fat
2   tablespoons green creme
    de menthe
2   tablespoons brown sugar

Mix ingredients well. Serve in a small bowl and garnish with a sprig of fresh mint. Good for a buffet with fresh fruit such as strawberries and melon balls. Makes enough for approximately 30 to 40 pieces of fruit.

Yield: ¾ cup

CITRUS DRESSING

Zest and Juice of one
   large lemon
Zest and juice of one large lime
Zest and juice of one
   large orange
1   cup fresh mint, chopped
3   tablespoons sugar

Combine all ingredients and mix well. Serve over any combination of fresh berries.

FRUIT SALAD DRESSING

½   pint whipping cream
¾   cup sugar
1   egg
    Juice of one lemon
    pinch of salt

In a small sauce pan, beat egg. Add sugar and salt and heat on stove. Add lemon juice and cook on medium-low. Stir constantly until thick like gravy. Cool completely. Whip cream separately and fold into mixture. It works well to make lemon mixture the day before and store in refrigerator.

This is a great addition to a fresh fruit salad and it's light tasting. Perfect for holiday dinners!

CAESAR SALAD DRESSING

¼	cup olive oil
	Juice of one lemon
¼	teaspoon Worcestershire sauce
2	cloves garlic, minced
	salt and pepper to taste

Combine all ingredients in a covered container and shake well. Serve with romain lettuce, parmesen cheese and croutons.

Dressing is best when added immediately before serving.

B'S HOMEMADE ONION MAYONNAISE

2	egg yolks
1	medium onion, quartered
1	teaspoon salt
2	tablespoons vinegar
3	tablespoons lemon juice
½	teaspoon ground red pepper
1	teaspoon paprika
1	teaspoon powdered mustard
2	cups salad oil

In a food processor, beat egg yolks. Add remaining ingredients except oil and beat until smooth. With the machine running, slowly add oil. Refrigerate for a few hours before serving.

This is great served with meats and on sandwiches!

Yield: 2 cups

JALAPEÑO-CILANTRO DRESSING

1	cup cilantro, chopped
¼	cup lime juice
2	cloves garlic, peeled
1	medium jalapeño, seeded and chopped
½	teaspoon salt
1	cup olive oil
½	cup plain yogurt

In a food processor, blend cilantro, lime juice, garlic, jalapeño and salt until smooth. With machine running, slowly add oil until well blended. Stir in yogurt and refrigerate.

Excellent on fruit salads as well as green salad. Can also be served beside fish and poultry.

Yield: 2 ½ cups

GARLIC FRENCH VINAIGRETTE

1	teaspoon garlic powder
1	cup heavy cream
1	teaspoon Dijon mustard
4	tablespoons champagne vinegar
4	tablespoons light olive oil

Whisk together all ingredients except oil. Slowly add oil and whisk until smooth. (Do not use a food processor as cream will chip and curdle.)

Use this dressing on Watercress-Blue Cheese Salad. (see page 49)

Yield: 2 cups

RASPBERRY VINAIGRETTE

1 ⅓	cups raspberry vinegar
1 ⅓	cups seedless raspberry jam
1	tablespoon coriander
2	teaspoons salt
1	teaspoon pepper
3	cups olive oil

Combine the first five ingredients in a blender or food processor and process until smooth. Slowly add oil in a stream and process until smooth. Store in refrigerator up to two weeks.

This dressing is great as a marinade for chicken or served on a fresh spinach salad!

Yield: 4 ½ cups

EASY BLUE CHEESE DRESSING

1	package ranch dressing mix
1	(4-ounce) package blue cheese, crumbled
½	teaspoon coarse black pepper

Prepare dressing according to package directions. Stir in blue cheese crumbles and pepper and refrigerate. If dressing becomes too thick, stir in small amount of half and half to desired consistency.

Yield: 2 ½ cups

CREAMY ROASTED RED PEPPER DRESSING

1	(7-ounce) jar roasted red peppers and juice
2	tablespoons red wine vinegar
2	green onions, finely chopped
½	teaspoon salt
½	teaspoon dried basil
1 ½	cups olive oil

In a food processor, combine all ingredients except oil. Blend until smooth. With machine running, slowly add oil and process until smooth and thick. Refrigerate.

Yield: 2 ⅔ cups

Red-crowned Parrots

Carolina Wren

Breakfast & Brunch

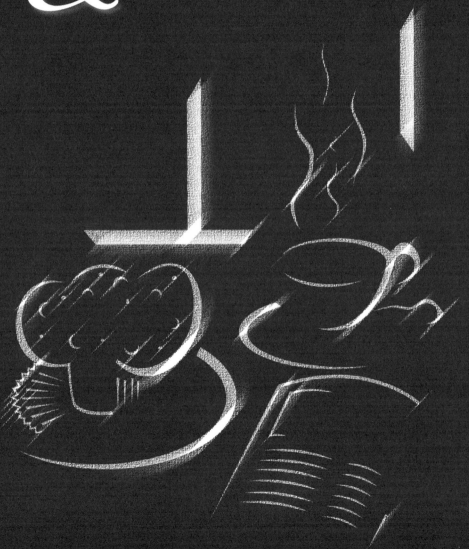

CHEESY BREAKFAST CASSEROLE

1	pound pork sausage (mild or hot)
⅔	cup milk
1	can cream of celery soup
3-4	eggs, beaten
2	cups frozen hashbrowns
1	cup Cheddar cheese, shredded
1	cup processed cheese, cubed

Fry sausage until crumbly and drain. Combine next five ingredients with sausage and pour into a 9 x 13-inch baking dish. Top with processed cheese. Bake at 350° for 45 minutes to one hour.

Yield: 8 servings

CHARITY BALL BREAKFAST CASSEROLE

6-7	slices sandwich bread
1	stick margarine
1	pound sausage, cooked and drained
1	(4-ounce) can chopped green chilis
1	cup Cheddar cheese, grated
5	eggs
½	pint milk
	dash Worcestershire sauce
1	teaspoon dry mustard
	dash salt and pepper
½	tablespoon minced onions

Trim crusts from bread and butter both sides. Press into a large 9 x 13-inch casserole dish. Top with cooked sausage, followed by the green chilis and cheese. In a blender, mix eggs, milk, Worcestershire sauce, dry mustard, salt, pepper and minced onions. Pour egg mixture over the cheese and cover with foil. Refrigerate overnight. Bake uncovered at 350° for 30 to 45 minutes.

Yield: 8-10 servings

SPINACH QUICHE

6-8   slices bacon, cooked
     and crumbled
1   box frozen spinach
4   ounces fresh mushrooms, sliced
     or 1 (4-ounce) jar sliced
     mushrooms
½   cup onion, chopped
½   cup bell pepper, chopped
2   eggs
¾   cup heavy cream
     dash ground nutmeg
1   cup Cheddar cheese, shredded
1   cup Monterey Jack cheese,
     shredded
2   tablespoons flour
1   (9-inch) deep dish pie shell

Sauté spinach, mushrooms, onion and bell pepper and season to taste. Beat eggs with cream and nutmeg and set aside. Mix cheeses with flour. Add bacon to pie shell. Layer one half of cheese mixture onto bacon. Add spinach mixture and then egg mixture. Top with remaining cheese. Bake at 350° for 30 minutes. Can be frozen before or after baking.

Yield: 6-8 servings

SURPRISE QUICHE

1   (9-inch) deep dish pie shell
2   teaspoons flour
1   cup Swiss, Cheddar or Monterey
     Jack cheese, shredded
2   eggs, beaten
½   cup mayonnaise
½   cup milk
6-8   slices bacon, cooked and crumbled
3   green onions, chopped

Partially bake pie crust at 400° for ten minutes. Toss cheeses and flour, and mix with eggs, milk and mayonnaise. Pour into pie shell and top with bacon and onions. Bake at 400° for 20 to 30 minutes or until firm and golden brown on top. May add mushrooms, broccoli or shrimp for variety.

Yield: 8-10 servings

SEAFOOD QUICHE

1	(6-ounce) package frozen crabmeat, thawed and drained	
1 ½	cups cooked shrimp, deveined and chopped	
1	cup Swiss cheese, shredded	
½	cup celery, finely chopped	
½	cup scallions, finely chopped	
2	(9-inch) deep dish pie shells	
1	cup mayonnaise	
2	tablespoons flour	
1	cup dry white wine	
4	eggs, slightly beaten	

Combine crabmeat, shrimp, cheese, celery and scallions. Divide mixture between two pie shells. Mix together mayonnaise, flour, wine and eggs. Pour half of mixture into each pie shell. Bake at 350° for 35 to 40 minutes. Can be frozen uncooked. Bake for 50 minutes if frozen.

Yield: 6-8 servings

SAUSAGE QUICHE

1	pound pork sausage, cooked, crumbled and drained
3	eggs, slightly beaten
½	cup milk
1	small jar mushrooms, drained
1 ½	cups Cheddar cheese, shredded
1	(9-inch) deep dish pie shell

Mix together sausage, eggs, milk, mushrooms and cheese. Pour egg mixture into pie shell. Bake at 400° for 30 minutes or until light brown.

Yield: 6-8 servings

BRUNCH QUICHE

1   (8-ounce) package cream
     cheese, cubed
1   cup milk
¼   cup onion, chopped
1   tablespoon margarine
4   eggs, beaten
1   cup ham, finely chopped
¼   cup pimiento, finely chopped
¼   teaspoon dill weed
     dash pepper
1   (10-inch) deep dish pie shell

Heat cream cheese and milk over low heat, stirring constantly until smooth. Sauté onions in margarine. In a large bowl, combine eggs and cream cheese mixture. Add onion, ham, pimiento and seasonings. Mix well. Pour into pie shell and bake at 350° for 35 to 40 minutes or until set. Garnish with ham and fresh dill.

Yield: 8 servings

SPINACH CHEESE SQUARES

2   (10-ounce) packages frozen
     chopped spinach, thawed
1   pound Cheddar cheese, shredded
3   eggs, beaten
1   cup milk
1   cup all purpose flour
1   teaspoon baking powder
1   tablespoon onion, chopped
½   teaspoon garlic powder
4   tablespoons butter

Blend all ingredients, except butter, in a large bowl. Melt butter in a 9 x 13-inch pan. Pour in mixture and bake at 350° for 30 minutes. Cut into one-inch squares when cool.

Yield: 24 servings

CRANBERRY NUT BREAD

1	cup sugar
½	teaspoon soda
2	cups flour
½	teaspoon salt
1 ½	teaspoon baking powder
2	tablespoons hot water
2	tablespoons shortening, melted
1	egg, beaten
½	cup orange juice
1	cup fresh cranberries, coarsely chopped
½	cup pecans, chopped

In a large bowl, mix the first five ingredients. Add other ingredients in the order listed. Bake in a greased loaf pan at 325° for one hour and ten minutes.

Yield: 1 loaf

PUMPKIN APPLE STREUSEL MUFFINS

2 ½	cups all-purpose flour
2	cups sugar
1	tablespoon pumpkin pie spice
1	teaspoon baking soda
½	teaspoon salt
2	eggs, slightly beaten
1	cup solid pack pumpkin
½	cup vegetable oil
2	cups apples, peeled and finely chopped

Streusel:

½	tablespoon flour
¼	cup sugar
½	teaspoon cinnamon
4	teaspoons butter, softened

In a large bowl, combine the first five ingredients and set aside. In a medium bowl, combine eggs, pumpkin and oil. Add liquid ingredients to the flour mixture and stir until moistened. Stir in apples. Spoon batter into greased muffin tins, filling ¾ full. In a small bowl, combine flour, sugar, cinnamon and butter and mix until crumbly. Sprinkle streusel topping over batter. Bake at 350° for 35 to 40 minutes or until toothpick comes out clean.

Yield: 2 dozen muffins

STRAWBERRY NUT BREAD

3	cups flour, sifted	
1	teaspoon soda	
1	teaspoon salt	
1	tablespoon cinnamon	
2	cups sugar	
4	eggs, beaten well	
1 ¼	cups vegetable oil	
2	cups strawberries, sliced (either fresh or frozen)	
1 ¼	cups pecans, chopped	

Sift together first five ingredients and set aside. In another bowl, mix eggs, oil, strawberries and pecans until well blended. Make a well in the center of the dry ingredients and add liquid mixture, stirring just enough to moisten the dry ingredients. Pour into six greased 6 x 3 x 2-inch foil pans or two 9 x 5 x 3-inch pans. Bake at 350° for 40 minutes for small pans and one hour for large pans. Remove from oven and cool on wire racks.

Yield: 6 small or 2 large loaves

PUMPKIN CARROT KAHLUA BREAD

3	cups brown sugar
3 ½	cups all-purpose flour
2	teaspoons baking soda
½	teaspoon salt
2	teaspoons nutmeg
2	teaspoons allspice
2	teaspoons cloves
2	teaspoons cinnamon
4	eggs
1	cup carrots, shredded
1	can pumpkin
1	cup oil
½	cup water
½	cup kahlua
1	cup pecans, chopped (optional)

Preheat oven to 325°. Grease large bundt pan and set aside. Combine sugar, flour, soda, salt and spices in a large bowl. In a separate large bowl, mix eggs, carrots, pumpkin, oil, water and kahlua. Combine liquid ingredients with the dry ingredients and mix well. Add nuts if desired. Bake one hour and 30 minutes or until an inserted toothpick comes out clean.

POPPYSEED BREAD

3 cups flour
2 ¼ cups sugar
3 eggs
1 ½ cups oil
1 ½ cups milk
1 ½ teaspoons salt
1 ½ teaspoons baking powder
1 ½ teaspoons vanilla
1 ½ teaspoons almond flavoring
1 ½ teaspoons butter flavoring
1 ½ tablespoons poppyseed

Glaze:
¼ cup orange or lemon juice
½ cup sugar
½ teaspoon each vanilla, almond, butter flavorings

Mix all but the last three ingredients in a large mixing bowl for three minutes. Grease and flour two large loaf pans or one bundt pan. Bake at 350° for one hour or more until done. Remove from pan. To prepare glaze, combine orange or lemon juice, sugar and vanilla, almond and butter flavorings in a saucepan. Cook for two to three minutes until sugar dissolves. Pour over hot bread.

BANANA BREAD

3 ripe bananas, mashed
1 cup sugar
1 egg
¼ cup butter, melted
1 ½ cups flour, sifted
1 teaspoon soda
½ teaspoon salt
½ cup pecans, optional

Combine bananas, sugar, egg and butter and mix well. Combine remaining three ingredients and add to banana mixture. Mix thoroughly until well blended. Pour into a greased loaf pan. Bake at 325° for one hour.

ICE BOX GINGER MUFFINS

1 ½ cups margarine, softened
1 cup sugar
½ cup dark corn syrup
½ cup molasses
4 large eggs
2 teaspoons baking soda
1 cup buttermilk
4 cups flour
⅛ teaspoon salt
2 teaspoons ginger
¼ teaspoon cinnamon
¼ teaspoon allspice
½ cup raisins, chopped
¾ cup pecans, chopped

Soften margarine and cream with sugar. Mix in syrup and molasses. Add eggs, one at a time. Stir soda into buttermilk and add to sugar mixture while it foams. Sift flour, salt and spices and slowly add it to the creamed mixture. (Butter may look a little curdled). Add raisins and nuts and store in a covered container in the refrigerator until ready to use. (May be kept up to six weeks.) Bake in greased or paper lined muffin pan at 400° for 12 to 15 minutes or until toothpick comes out clean.

CREAM CHEESE CRESCENTS

2 cans crescent rolls
2 (8-ounce) packages cream cheese
1 egg, separated into yolk
  and white
1 cup sugar
1 teaspoon vanilla

Icing:
1 cup powdered sugar
2 tablespoons milk
½ teaspoon vanilla

In a buttered 9 x 13-inch glass baking dish, spread out one can of crescent rolls, pinching seams together. Cream together the cream cheese, egg yolk, sugar and vanilla and spread on the dough. Top with another can of rolls. Pinch seams and sides together. Fork whip egg white and brush on top. Bake at 350° for 30 minutes. Mix together the powdered sugar, milk and vanilla until well blended. Ice the crescents when they are cool.

CINNAMON ROLLS

¼	cup milk
¼	cup sugar
1	teaspoon salt
3	tablespoons butter
1	package dry yeast
¼	cup warm water
2 ¼	cups flour, divided
1	egg
2	tablespoons butter, softened
¼	cup brown sugar
½	teaspoon cinnamon
½	cup raisins or blueberries
½	cup pecans
1	tablespoon butter, melted

Icing:

1	cup powdered sugar
2	tablespoons milk

Combine first four ingredients in a saucepan. Heat until butter melts and cool to 105 - 115° (using a candy thermometer). Dissolve yeast in warm water in a large mixing bowl and let stand five minutes. Stir in sugar/milk mixture, 1 ½ cup flour and egg. Beat at medium speed until smooth and stir in remaining ¾ cup flour. Turn dough out on a lightly floured surface and knead until smooth and elastic (about eight minutes). Place in a well greased bowl, turning once. Cover and let rise in a warm place for one hour (dough will not quite double). Punch dough down. Turn dough out onto a lightly floured surface. Roll into a 12 x 8 rectangle and spread with 2 tablespoons of softened butter. Combine brown sugar, pecans and cinnamon and sprinkle mixture over rectangle. Sprinkle with raisins or blueberries if desired. Roll dough into a jelly roll, starting at the long side. Pinch seam to seal but do not seal ends. Cut roll into 1 inch slices and place the slices cut side down in a greased 8-inch square pan. Brush tops with one tablespoon melted butter. Using a fork, gently lift center of rolls to form a peak. Cover and let rise for approximately 40 minutes. Bake at 350° for 35 minutes. To glaze, combine sugar and 2 tablespoons of warm milk, stirring well. Drizzle over warm rolls.

GEORGE'S PANCAKES WITH HOT MAPLE SYRUP

1	cup flour
½	teaspoon salt
1 ½	tablespoons sugar
½	teaspoon soda
1	egg, beaten
1	cup buttermilk
1	tablespoon corn oil

Sift together the dry ingredients and mix with a fork In a separate bowl, beat egg and add buttermilk and oil. Blend well. Add to dry ingredients, mixing with a fork. Be sure to leave a few lumps. Spoon pancakes onto a hot griddle set at 350°. Serve with butter and Hot Maple Syrup.

Hot Maple Syrup:

1 ¼	cups light corn syrup
½	cup brown sugar
¼	cup water
	maple flavoring (to taste)
1	tablespoon butter

Combine the first three ingredients in a saucepan over medium low heat until sugar dissolves. Add a few drops of maple flavoring and butter. Serve over George's Pancakes.

FANCY FRENCH TOAST

12	eggs
⅓	cup maple syrup
2	cups milk
12	slices bread
2	(8-ounce) packages cream cheese

In a large bowl, beat the eggs and combine with maple syrup and milk. Break bread into bite size pieces and distribute evenly into a 9 x 13-inch baking dish. Cut up cream cheese and sprinkle over the bread. Pour egg mixture over bread and cream cheese and cover with plastic wrap. Refrigerate overnight. Bake at 375° for 45 minutes.

MRS. RAIMOND'S REFRIGERATOR ROLLS

1	package or 1 tablespoon of dry active yeast
½	cup warm water
½	cup shortening
½	cup plus 1 tablespoon sugar
1	egg, beaten
2	cups hot water
1 ½	teaspoons salt
6	cups flour
½	cup butter, melted

Dissolve the yeast in ½ cup warm water. Add one tablespoon of sugar. Cover and allow to proof. (It will grow thicker and bubbly as the yeast is working. If nothing happens, throw away and start over.) In two cups of hot water, melt the shortening. Add the ½ cup sugar, beaten egg, softened yeast and salt. Add the flour one cup at a time until a soft, runny dough forms. Knead just a little with some additional flour. Put the dough in a large greased pottery bowl and flip over so that the top is greased. Cover with plastic wrap and refrigerate for many hours until doubled or tripled. Once the dough has risen sufficiently, roll it out on a flour surface to about ¼ to ½ inch. Cut with a glass or biscuit cutter. Dip quickly in melted butter and fold in half. Place in a 9 x 13-inch pan, touching but not packed. Let rise for two and a half to three hours. Bake in a 400° oven for 10-15minutes.

Yield: 2 dozen rolls

Entrées

MUSHROOM STUFFED TENDERLOIN
WITH RED BELL PEPPER SAUCE

5 tablespoons butter
1 cup red bell pepper, chopped
¼ cup shallot, minced
¼ pound fresh shitake or other
mushrooms, minced
¼ teaspoon salt
1 (3 ½ - 4 pound) beef tenderloin
olive oil
salt and pepper

Red Bell Pepper Sauce:
1 ½ cups red bell pepper, chopped
7 tablespoons beef broth
1 ½ teaspoons fresh lemon juice
1 stick butter, cut into tablespoons
2 tablespoons sour cream,
room-temperature
salt and pepper

Melt butter in heavy skillet over medium heat. Add bell pepper and shallots. Cook until softened, about five minutes. Mix in mushrooms and salt. Can be prepared a day ahead of time and refrigerated.

Cut tenderloin in half lengthwise. Cut a one inch wide pocket lengthwise down the middle of each half. Stuff each pocket with half of bell pepper mixture. Seal pockets with toothpicks. Brush beef with olive oil. Season with salt and pepper to taste. Roast at 400° for 25 minutes until medium-rare. Let stand ten minutes. Cut into 1 ½ inch slices.

To prepare sauce, cook bell pepper and four tablespoons of the broth in a saucepan over medium heat until all liquid is evaporated. Transfer to food processor. Add remaining three tablespoons of broth and lemon juice and puree. Strain through fine sieve into saucepan. Set over low heat. Whisk in butter one tablespoon at a time. Whisk in sour cream. Sauce can be prepared a day ahead of time and refrigerated. Serve with tenderloin.

Yield: 8 servings

LOBSTER STUFFED TENDERLOIN

2	(4-ounce) lobster tails
1	(3- 4 pound) tenderloin, butterflied
1	tablespoon butter, melted
1 ½	teaspoon fresh lemon juice
6	strips bacon, partially cooked
½	cup green onion, chopped
½	cup butter
½	cup dry white wine
⅛	teaspoon garlic powder

Cook lobsters in simmering water five to six minutes. Remove from shell. Split tenderloin lengthwise. Place lobster end to end inside beef. Drizzle butter and lemon juice over lobster. Tie meat with kitchen string at one to two inch intervals. Place on rack in shallow pan. Roast at 425° for 40 to 45 minutes. Place bacon on top and cook and additional five minutes. Sauté onion in butter. Add wine and garlic powder. Slice roast and serve with butter sauce.

ROUND STEAK DELUXE

1 ½	pounds tenderized round steak
1	teaspoon olive oil
⅓	package dried onion soup mix
¼	cup celery, chopped
¼	teaspoon celery salt
¼	teaspoon garlic powder
10	fresh mushrooms, sliced
½	(15-ounce) can diced tomatoes
¼	cup cooking wine
4	Roma tomatoes, sliced
½	teaspoon oregano
½	medium onion, chopped
4	medium potatoes, peeled and sliced lengthwise into four quarters

Cut round steak into serving-size pieces. In a Dutch oven, lightly brown pieces in oil. Add the rest of the ingredients, except potatoes. Add enough water to barely cover meat and vegetables. Bring to a boil. Cover and simmer about 30 minutes, stirring occasionally. Add potatoes on top, but not immersed in the liquid. Cover and cook at a low simmer about one and a half to two hours, until steak is tender and potatoes are cooked.

Yield: 4 servings.

BAKED SWEDISH MEATBALLS

1 ¼	pounds lean ground beef	Mix all ingredients together well.
1	onion, minced	Form into small balls. Dip into flour.
½	green pepper, minced	Brown in a small amount of oil in
1	egg	large skillet. Drain meatballs, reserv-
1	tablespoon Worcestershire sauce	ing two tablespoons of drippings.
1 ½	tablespoon catsup	Place in a 9 X 13-inch baking dish.
½	teaspoon garlic salt	
	salt and pepper	
	flour	
	oil	

Gravy:

2	tablespoons flour	To prepare gravy, add flour to drip-
2	tablespoons oil from skillet	pings. Add water, Worcestershire
2	cups water	sauce, and catsup. Pour gravy over
4	tablespoons Worcestershire sauce	meatballs. Bake at 325° about 45 min-
4	tablespoons catsup	utes. Serve over rice, noodles, or
		spaghetti.

BEST MEAT LOAF

½	cup tomato catsup	In a large bowl, combine all ingredi-
⅓	cup tomato juice	ents, except beef. Mix thoroughly.
½	teaspoon salt	Add ground beef. Mix gently, but
½	teaspoon pepper	thoroughly. Press beef mixture into a
⅛	teaspoon red pepper	9 X 5-inch loaf pan.
2	eggs, beaten	
¾	cup fresh bread crumbs	In a separate bowl, combine catsup,
¼	cup onions, finely chopped	mustard and brown sugar. Mix well.
2	teaspoons prepared mustard	Spread mixture over meat loaf. Bake
1 ½	pounds lean ground beef	at 400° for 35 to 40 minutes or until
½	cup tomato catsup	done. Drain off fat. Let meat loaf set
1	teaspoon prepared mustard	five minutes before serving.
4	teaspoons brown sugar	Yield: 4-5 servings.

OVEN BRISKET

1	(3 - 7 pound) beef brisket
⅓	cup Worcestershire sauce
⅔	cup water
½	package onion soup mix
½	large onion, sliced

Sear meat on a hot grill or in a large skillet for approximately ten minutes on each side. Put meat in a large oven bag and pour on worcestershire sauce and water. Sprinkle with onion soup mix and top with onion slices. Close bag with a tie and place in a broiler pan. Cook at 200-250° for six to eight hours. Juice left in bag can be thickened with cornstarch and used as gravy.

CORNISH ITALIANO

2	Cornish game hens, halved
1 ½	teaspoons sage
1	teaspoon rosemary
1	teaspoon garlic powder
1	teaspoon salt
⅛	teaspoon pepper
2	tablespoons butter
2	tablespoons olive oil
1	cup dry white wine
2	tablespoons flour
½	cup water
¾	cup sour cream
¼	cup Parmesan cheese
8	ounces medium egg noodles

Mix dry seasonings. Rub hens with seasonings inside and out. In a Dutch oven melt butter and oil. Brown hens on all sides. Add wine. Cover. Simmer 45 minutes until tender. Remove hens to a warm plate. Mix flour and water. Add to pan juices for sauce. Cook egg noodles in a separate pan. Drain and mix in sour cream and parmesan cheese. Place hens on noodles and top with sauce.

Yield: 4 servings

HOMESTYLE SPAGHETTI
AND MEATBALLS

1	pound ground chuck
1	teaspoon vegetable oil
½	cup onion, finely chopped
½	cup parsley, finely chopped
¼	teaspoon garlic powder
½	cup fresh, unseasoned bread crumbs
1	egg, lightly beaten
	salt and pepper to taste
1	tablespoon olive oil
1	cup onion, finely chopped
1	teaspoon garlic, finely minced
1	(28-ounce) can crushed or stewed tomatoes, preferably imported
1	teaspoon tomato paste
½	teaspoon rosemary
¼	teaspoon marjoram
¼	teaspoon oregano
¼	teaspoon hot pepper flakes, optional
1	pound spaghetti
1	tablespoon butter
	salt and pepper to taste
	grated Parmesan, optional

Place meat in a mixing bowl and set aside. In a small skillet, heat vegetable oil and cook onion until translucent and wilted. Remove from heat and set aside to cool slightly. Add cooked onions to meat. Add parsley, garlic powder, bread crumbs, egg, salt and pepper. Blend well with your hands. Shape the meat mixture into approximately 16 meatballs. In a large skillet, heat olive oil and add meatballs. Turn them as needed to brown evenly, about five minutes. Spoon out any excess fat in skillet. Scatter one cup onions and garlic around meatballs and saute lightly until almost translucent. Add crushed tomatoes, tomato paste, rosemary, marjoram, oregano, hot pepper flakes, salt and pepper. Bring to a boil. Lower heat to medium. Cover and simmer about 20 minutes. In a large stockpot, boil water for pasta. Cook spaghetti to desired doneness, preferably "al dente". Drain and place spaghetti back in pot. Add butter, salt and pepper to taste and toss well. Serve the spaghetti in pasta bowls with meatballs and sauce. Sprinkle with parmesan cheese, if desired.

Yield: 4 servings

ITALIAN SAUSAGE, PEPPER AND ONIONS

1	pound Italian sausage links
1-2	large green peppers
1-2	large onions
4	cups tomato sauce
	Linguini, Spaghetti or other pasta

Sauté Italian sausage over medium heat in a non-stick saucepan. Cook until well heated through, about 30 minutes. Slice peppers and onions lengthwise. Add peppers, onions and tomato sauce to pan. Cover and cook over low heat for one to two hours, until vegetables are soft. Serve over cooked pasta.

Yield: 6 servings

LUSCIOUS LASAGNA

1 ½	pounds sweet Italian sausage
	olive oil
2-3	cloves garlic, minced
4-6	ounces sliced fresh mushrooms, sliced
½	cup onion, chopped
½	cup bell pepper, chopped
2	tablespoons fresh parsley, chopped
2	tablespoons fresh basil, chopped
2	tablespoons fresh oregano or 1 teaspoon dry
1	(6-ounce) can tomato paste
1	(28-ounce) can whole tomatoes
1	(8-ounce) can tomato sauce
1 ½	cups water
2	(16-ounce) containers Ricotta cheese
2	eggs, slightly beaten
1	cup fresh grated Parmesan cheese
1	teaspoon salt
¼	teaspoon pepper
2	tablespoons fresh parsley, chopped
1	pound sliced Mozzarella cheese
	lasagna noodles, cooked

To prepare meat sauce, brown sausage in a little olive oil. Add minced garlic, onion, bell pepper, mushrooms, parsley, basil and oregano. Season with salt and pepper. Add tomato paste. Heat through. Add tomatoes with the juice. Break up tomatoes in the pan. Add tomato sauce and water. Let simmer. In large bowl, blend Ricotta cheese, eggs, Parmesan cheese, salt, pepper and parsley. In a 16 X 12-inch dish, layer noodles, cheese mixture, mozzarella and meat mixture. Repeat in that order. Bake uncovered at 350° for 30 minutes.

Yield: 8-10 servings

Translated on page 226

PASTA PUTTANESCA

1	pound spaghetti or linguini	
2	(2 pound) cans peeled Italian plum tomatoes	
¼	cup olive oil	
1	teaspoon oregano	
⅛	teaspoon dried red pepper flakes	
½	cup tiny black Nicoise olives	
¼	cup drained capers	
4	garlic cloves, peeled and chopped	
8	anchovy fillets, coarsely chopped	
½	cup chopped Italian parsley, plus some for garnish	
2	tablespoons salt	

Bring four quarts water to a boil in a large pot. Add salt and stir in spaghetti. Cook until tender, but still firm. Drain immediately and transfer to four heated plates. While spaghetti is cooking, drain tomatoes and cut crosswise into halves, squeezing out as much liquid as possible. Combine tomatoes and olive oil in a skillet and bring to a boil. Keeping the sauce at a full boil, add remaining ingredients, except pasta. Stir frequently. Reduce heat slightly. Continue to cook for a few minutes, or until sauce has thickened to your liking. Serve immediately over hot pasta and garnish with additional parsley.

Yield: 4 servings

Rio Fest is the party Harlingen throws each year for itself! The dream of a six-member committee of the Harlingen Junior Service League, Rio Fest was launched in 1982 and attracted over 20,000 visitors that first year with food, music, and more. Today, the festival is co-sponsored by the Harlingen Junior League, the city of Harlingen and the Harlingen Area Chamber of Commerce, and has an unpaid staff of over 2,000 volunteers. Emphasizing the cultural diversity of the Valley, Rio Fest features art exhibits, music, and dance programs, professional and amateur quality entertainment, good food and a popular children's area.

BAKED TORTELLINI WITH EGGPLANT AND POTATOES

½   pound eggplant, diced into
      ¾-inch pieces
½   pound tortellini filled with
      beef or cheese
½   pound potatoes, peeled and
      cut into ¾-inch slices
½   cup olive oil or as needed
1   onion, thinly sliced
1   (14-ounce) can Italian peeled or
      stewed tomatoes
½   teaspoon fresh chopped oregano
      or ¼ teaspoon dried
      pinch cayenne pepper
      salt to taste
      fresh ground black
      pepper to taste
1   cup Fontina or Mozzarella
      cheese, shredded
3   tablespoons fresh chopped
      oregano or parsley

Translated on page 227

Sprinkle eggplant with salt and leave to drain over sink in a colander or drainer. Boil tortellini. Drain. Place in a shallow 9-inch dish or quiche pan. In a small saucepan, boil potatoes until just cooked. Drain. Heat some oil in a frying pan. Sauté potatoes until brown. Add to the tortellini. With a little more oil, sauté onion gently for about five minutes. Add drained eggplant. Continue cooking, adding more oil if necessary, until eggplant is tender and golden. Lightly drain tomatoes and add to eggplant mixture, breaking up with a spoon. Add oregano, cayenne, salt and pepper. Cook five to eight minutes more, or until tomatoes have reduced and there is little liquid left. Add to tortellini and potatoes and toss with ⅓ of cheese. Season with salt and pepper. Top with remaining cheese. Sprinkle with extra oregano or parsley. Bake at 375° for ten minutes uncovered or until cheese melt and bubbles. Does not freeze well.

Yield: 4 servings

ITALIAN TOMATO SAUCE

3-4 cloves garlic, finely chopped
2 tablespoons onion, finely chopped
1 tablespoon olive oil
1 (28-ounce) can whole tomatoes, chopped well
1 (8-ounce) can tomato sauce
1 (6-ounce) can tomato paste
1 teaspoon oregano
1 teaspoon red pepper,crushed
1 teaspoon basil
⅓ cup dry red wine, if desired
½ teaspoon sugar

Sauté garlic and onion with olive oil in a saucepan about five to ten minutes, or until tender. Add tomatoes. Stir well. Add remaining ingredients. Bring to a boil. Simmer, covered, over low heat for three to four hours.

Serve over pasta or use in other recipes. Freezes well up to six months.

GERMAN SAUERBRATEN

1 (3-pound) beef pot roast
½ cup vinegar
½ cup water
1 small onion, chopped
2 bay leaves, broken
3 whole cloves garlic
2 teaspoons salt
  fat from roasting pan

Place the roast into a non-metal bowl and add vinegar, water, onion, bay leaves, cloves and salt. Refrigerate for at least twenty-four hours. Remove the beef from the liquid. Place in oven and roast at 325°. When partly done, pour the liquid back on and continue to roast for two to three more hours. After the roast is done, remove from liquid and make gravy. Add more water if necessary.

REUBEN CASSEROLE

1	(8-ounce) carton sour cream	Combine sour cream and minced
¼	cup onion, minced	onion. Layer sour cream, sauerkraut,
1	(1-pound) can sauerkraut	corn beef, Swiss cheese and rye bread.
1	can corn beef, crumbled	Drizzle butter on top. Bake at 350° for
2	cups Swiss cheese,	45 minutes.
	shredded	
7	slices rye bread, cubed	
1	cup margarine, melted	

BEST HOMEMADE PIZZA

1	pound ground beef	Grease pizza or jelly roll pan. Brown
1	(8-ounce) can tomato sauce	ground beef and drain. Stir in tomato
¼	cup water	sauce, water and seasoning mix,
1	envelope Italian style spaghetti	reserving one tablespoon of mix for
	sauce mix, reserve 1 tablespoon	the crust. Simmer while preparing
1	package hot roll mix	crust. In a large bowl, dissolve yeast
1	cup warm water	from hot roll mix in warm water. Add
1	(4-ounce) package Mozzarella	reserved sauce mix and hot roll flour
	cheese, shredded	mixture. Blend well. Press dough in

pan forming a high rim around the
edge. Spread meat mixture over
dough. Bake on low rack at 400° for
25 to 30 minutes until brown.
Sprinkle with cheese and other
cheeses if you like. Bake another two
to three minutes until cheese melts.

HAM LOAF WITH MUSTARD HORSERADISH SAUCE

1	cup milk
1	cup dry bread crumbs
2	eggs, beaten
2	pounds ground smoked ham
1 ½	pounds ground pork
1	tablespoon dried onion flakes
¾	cup brown sugar
¼	cup water
¼	cup vinegar
2	teaspoons dry mustard
⅛	teaspoon allspice

Mustard Horseradish Sauce:

¼	cup prepared horseradish
1 ½	tablespoons vinegar
1	tablespoon prepared mustard
¼	teaspoon Worcestershire sauce
	dash cayenne pepper
	dash paprika
½	pint whipping cream, whipped

Combine milk and crumbs. Add eggs, meat and onions. Mix well. Pack into a well-greased loaf pan or ring mold. Invert into a shallow baking pan. Bake at 350° for one and a half hours. Mix brown sugar, water, vinegar, dry mustard and allspice. Whisk to blend. Baste loaf occasionally with sauce until it is all used. To make Mustard Horseradish sauce, blend horseradish, vinegar, mustard, Worcestershire sauce, cayenne pepper and paprika. Fold into whipping cream. Chill. Serve over ham loaf.

Yield: 10-12 servings

The Harlingen Independent School District recently became the first District in the State to win both Honor School Board of Texas and Texas Superintendent of the Year. The system has an enrollment of over 16,000 students and the high performance of these students greatly assisted Harlingen in being named All America City. Eight private and parochial schools also serve the needs of local students.

RIO GRANDE PORK CHOPS

4   boneless pork loin chops, ½ to ¼ inch thick, trim fat
1   tablespoon oil
1   clove garlic, minced
2   teaspoons oil
4   tablespoons dry sherry
2   tablespoons soy sauce
2   tablespoons brown sugar
½   teaspoon crushed red pepper
2   teaspoons cornstarch
2   tablespoons water
     angel hair pasta for 4

Heat skillet and add oil. Brown pork chops on both sides. Remove. Add a bit more oil if needed. Sauté garlic for about one minute, (be careful not to burn it). Combine oil, sherry, soy sauce, brown sugar and crushed red pepper. Return chops to skillet and cover with sauce. Cover. Simmer over low heat, turning once, about 30 to 35 minutes, or until chops are tender and cooked through. (Add one to two tablespoons water if needed to keep sauce from cooking down too much.) Remove chops. Stir in cornstarch dissolved in water. Cook sauce until thickened. To serve, place angel hair pasta in deep serving dish. Arrange chops on top of pasta. Pour sauce over chops. Serve immediately.

Yield: 4-6 servings

PORK AND SQUASH

2   pounds pork steaks or roast, cubed
1   onion, diced
1   clove garlic, crushed
     pinch of ground cumin
3   sprigs coriander
1   tomato, diced
1   (15-ounce) can whole kernel corn
6   baby squash, sliced

Translated on page 228

Brown the pork until medium cooked. Add the onion, garlic, cumin, coriander and tomato. Saute on lower heat. Add the corn, squash and a little water. Cook about two to three minutes or until squash is tender.

Yield: 4-6 servings

STUFFED PORK TENDERLOIN

1-2   pound pork tenderloin
½   pound ground sausage
     salt and pepper
2   tablespoons unsalted butter

Sauce:
2   tablespoons oil
1   cup mushrooms, sliced
½   cup scallions, sliced
2   tablespoons flour
1 ½   cups warm milk
2   tablespoons coarse-grain mustard

Translated on page 225

Split tenderloin lengthwise. Stuff tenderloin with sausage. Tie meat with kitchen string at one to two inch intervals. Salt and pepper tenderloin to taste. Melt butter in saute´ pan. Add tenderloin and brown. Place browned tenderloin in roasting pan. Roast at 350° for 30 to 40 minutes to an internal temperature of 170°. To prepare sauce, in a sauté pan heat the oil. Sauté mushrooms and scallions for five minutes. Stir in flour. Add warm milk and whisk to a thick sauce. Blend in mustard. Remove cooked tenderloin. Remove string and slice in ½-inch circles. Arrange on a serving platter. Drizzle sauce over meat.

I n 1968, the city of Harlingen donated land and buildings of the former Harlingen Air Force Base to what is today known as Texas State Technical College. Harlingen has continued to support the school with additional land and major funding for building construction. Through close collaboration with business, industry, governmental agencies and communities, TSTC has become a highly effective technical educational system.

FANCY WINE CHICKEN

4   boneless chicken breasts
6   tablespoons all-purpose flour
¼   teaspoon pepper
¼   teaspoon paprika
4   tablespoons butter or margarine
¾   cup white wine or water
1 ¼   teaspoons chicken bouillon
¼   teaspoon poultry seasoning
1 ¾   cups mushrooms, sliced
½   cup onion, diced
¾   cup celery, diced
½   cup carrots, diced
½   cup sour cream
       chopped parsley for garnish

Trim any skin that may be left on chicken breasts. Mix flour, pepper and paprika in a plastic bag. Place chicken in bag, one breast at a time, and shake to coat. Save flour mixture to use later. Melt two tablespoons butter in large frying pan until it bubbles. Brown chicken breasts on both sides on medium heat. Set chicken aside. Melt remaining butter in pan. Stir in remaining flour mixture until butter is absorbed. Add wine and stir until smooth. Stir in chicken bouillon, poultry seasoning, mushrooms, onions, celery and carrots. Add chicken to mixture. Cover and simmer for 25 minutes. Remove only the chicken and place on plate. Stir sour cream into pan. Cook on medium heat until heated through. Pour sauce over chicken, sprinkle with parsley and serve.

Yield: 4 servings

LEMON DILL CHICKEN

½   cup dry bread crumbs
1 ½   teaspoons lemon-pepper
       seasoning
½   teaspoon dried dillweed
6   skinless, boneless, chicken breast
       halves
1   egg, beaten
2   tablespoons vegetable oil

Combine first three ingredients in a shallow dish. Dip chicken in egg and dredge in crumb mixture. Heat oil in large skillet over medium heat. Add chicken and cook five minutes on each side or until golden brown. Cover and cook for five more minutes.

Yield: 6 servings

CHICKEN AND DRESSING CASSEROLE

6-8	skinless, boneless chicken breasts	
3-4	slices mild Swiss cheese	
1	can cream of chicken soup	
½	cup sherry	
¼	cup half and half	
1	tablespoon ground sage	
	half of package herbed stuffing	
¾	stick butter, melted	

Lay chicken breasts in a large, flat casserole. Top each with a half slice of Swiss cheese. Mix cream of chicken soup, sherry and half and half. Pour mixture over chicken. Add sage to half a bag of stuffing. Mix well. Sprinkle on top of soup mixture. Pour butter on top of stuffing. Bake uncovered at 350° for one hour.

Yield: 6-8 servings

CITRUS CHICKEN

3	skinless, boneless chicken breasts
¼	cup butter, melted
2	tablespoons orange liqueur
6	thin slices cooked ham
	flour
2	eggs, slightly beaten
1	cup fine dry breadcrumbs
½	stick butter, cut into bits
1	tablespoon tarragon
1	teaspoon orange peel, grated
½	teaspoon salt
2	cups fresh orange juice

Brush one side of chicken with melted butter and liqueur. Place one slice of ham on each breast. Roll up and secure with toothpicks. Roll in flour. Dip in beaten egg, then roll in bread crumbs. Arrange in a shallow buttered baking dish. Dot with butter bits. Bake at 400° for 15 minutes. Mix together orange juice, tarragon, orange peel and salt. Pour over chicken. Reduce oven temperature to 350° and bake 35 minutes longer.

Yield: 6 servings

POPPY SEED CHICKEN

1	whole chicken, cooked, boned and cut into pieces
1	(8-ounce) carton sour cream
1	can cream of chicken soup
2	tablespoons poppy seeds
1	bag round buttery crackers, crushed
1	stick butter, melted

Place chicken pieces in a casserole dish. Mix sour cream and chicken soup. Pour over chicken. Combine poppy seeds, crackers and butter in a bowl. Spread cracker mixture on top. Bake at 350° for 30 to 40 minutes.

Yield: 6-8 servings

KALIMANTAN ISLAND CHICKEN

1	(8-ounce) can pineapple chunks
2	pounds chicken, cut into chunks
2	tablespoons shortening
1	can chicken broth
¼	cup vinegar
2	tablespoons pineapple syrup
2	teaspoons soy sauce
1	large clove garlic, minced
1	medium bell pepper, cut in squares
3	tablespoons cornstarch
¼	cup water

Drain pineapple into a bowl. Reserve syrup and chunks for later. Brown chicken in oil. Add broth, vinegar, syrup, soy sauce and garlic. Cover. Cook over low heat for 40 minutes. Add green pepper and pineapple. Cook five more minutes, stirring occasionally. Combine cornstarch and water. Stir into chicken mixture. Cook over low heat until thickened. Serve with rice.

GREEK FETA CHICKEN

1   cup plain non-fat or low-fat
     yogurt
1   large clove garlic, minced
½   teaspoon dried oregano,
     crumbled
¼   teaspoon pepper
4   bonelesss, skinless chicken breast
     halves
⅓   cup Feta cheese, crumbled
     fresh parsley sprigs

Whisk first four ingredients in medium bowl. Add chicken and turn to coat. Cover and let stand 30 minutes. Preheat broiler. Line broiler pan with foil. Remove chicken from marinade and place smooth side down on prepared pan, reserving marinade in bowl. Broil chicken six minutes. Turn chicken over. Brush with reserved marinade. Sprinkle with cheese. Broil until chicken is cooked through, about four minutes. Transfer to plates and garnish with parsley.

Yield: 4 servings

CHICKEN WITH ARTICHOKES AND TOMATOES

4   chicken breasts
     seasoned flour
     oil
¾   cup chicken broth
¾   cup white wine
1   (15-ounce) can artichoke hearts
1   (14-ounce) can tomatoes
5   green onions, chopped
½   green pepper, chopped

Translated on page 229

Dredge chicken in seasoned flour. Brown slowly in oil about ten to 15 minutes. Reduce heat. Add broth and wine. Cover and cook for 30 minutes. Add artichokes, tomatoes, onions and green peppers. Cook for another five to ten minutes. Serve with rice.

Yield: 4 servings

CHICKEN CORDON BLEU

1   pound boneless, skinless chicken breasts, pounded very thin
6   ounces ham, very thinly sliced
6   ounces Swiss cheese, very thinly sliced
½   cup flour
1-2   eggs, beaten
1 ½   cups seasoned dry breadcrumbs
½   cup oil

Mushroom Sauce:

1   package mushroom sauce mix
½   pound mushrooms, sliced
1   tablespoon butter
1   cup heavy cream
½   cup dry white wine
2   ounces Swiss cheese

Translated on page 231

Take chicken breast and place a slice of ham and a cheese slice in middle and roll up tightly. Secure with toothpicks. Repeat. Dip chicken rolls in flour to coat. Dip in eggs. (For a thicker crust, repeat coatings.) Coat thoroughly with breadcrumbs. Heat oil in a nonstick skillet. Fry chicken rolls in pan, turning occasionally about 20 minutes or until browned. Place in a 16 X 9-inch baking pan. Bake covered at 350° for 15 minutes.

To prepare mushroom sauce, mix all ingredients in a saucepan. Simmer 30 minutes or until heated through.

Add mushroom sauce to chicken. Bake covered for 30 minutes. Remove cover. Bake ten more minutes. Serve with mashed potatoes.

Fields of spiky-leaved aloe vera... called "the plant of immortality" by ancient Egyptians... are a common sight in the Rio Grande Valley, home to 99 percent of all aloe vera grown in the U.S. Scientifically speaking, the clear gel from this subtropical succulent is an ingenious combination of astringent, antibiotic and coagulating agents that ease pain, prevent scars and stimulate growth. What South Texas homemakers have traditionally used for centuries, lately has become a marketable ingredient in everything from shampoos to diaper wipes.

CHICKEN PARMESAN

1	pound boneless, skinless chicken breasts
½	cup flour
2-3	eggs, beaten
1 ½	cups Italian style breadcrumbs
¼	tablespoon olive oil
2-3	cups prepared tomato sauce
8	ounces Mozzarella cheese, shredded
4	ounces Swiss cheese, shredded
	spaghetti or linguini

Coat chicken pieces with flour. Dip in eggs. (For a thicker crust, repeat flour and egg coating.) Roll in breadcrumbs on both sides. Heat oil in a non-stick skillet. Cook chicken on medium heat for about 20 minutes, turning once. Drain on paper towels to remove excess oil. Spread thin layer of tomato sauce in a 16 X 9-inch baking dish. Add chicken in a single layer. Cover with remaining tomato sauce and both cheeses. Bake covered at 350° about 30 minutes. Remove cover and bake an additional ten minutes or until cheese is bubbly. Serve with spaghetti. Can substitute veal for chicken.

Yield: 8 servings

CHICKEN TETRAZZINI

4	boneless, skinless chicken breast halves
½	stick butter or margarine
1	small onion, sliced
1	can cream of chicken or cream of mushroom soup
8	ounces American cheese
4	ounces cream cheese
½	cup milk
3	tablespoons sweet pimientos, chopped
	salt and pepper to taste
1	large package egg noodles

Cook chicken and cut into bite size pieces. Melt butter in a large pot or skillet. Saute onion until tender. Add soup, cheeses and milk. Simmer on low heat until smooth. Add chicken and pimentos. Season with salt and pepper. (Extra milk or water can be added if mixture seems too thick.) Cook and drain noodles. Sauce can be mixed with noodles and baked in a casserole until bubbly or poured over noodles on individual plates.

Yield: 4 servings

CHICKEN LINGUINI

1	whole chicken
12	ounces linguini
2	(5-ounce) cans evaporated milk
2	cream of chicken soup
1	stick butter, melted
8	ounces cheddar or Colby cheese, shredded

Translated on page 230

Boil chicken in water 30 minutes. When done, remove chicken and reserve stock. Boil linguini in stock according to package directions. Debone chicken and cut into bite sized pieces. Mix evaporated milk, chicken soup and butter together in a bowl. Add chicken and linguini. Pour into a large casserole and top with cheese. Bake at 350° for 20 to 30 minutes or until bubbly. For a variety, spice up this dish by adding ½ cup sauteed onions, 1 cup mushrooms, 2 teaspoons garlic salt and 2 teaspoons cayenne pepper.

PASTA WITH CHICKEN AND SUN-DRIED TOMATOES

¼	cup oil
3	large boneless chicken breasts, cut into one-inch cubes
1	onion, chopped
1	clove garlic, chopped
½	teaspoon Fennel seeds
1	carrot, peeled and cut into matchstick-sized strips
¼	cup oil-packed sun-dried tomatoes, drained and finely chopped
12	ounces fettucine, freshly cooked
1	cup fresh Parmesan cheese, grated

Translated on page 229

Heat oil in heavy, large skillet over medium high heat. Add chicken and saute about six minutes or until brown and cooked through. Using slotted spoon, transfer chicken to a large bowl. Keep warm. Add onion, garlic and Fennel seeds to skillet. Saute onions about six minutes or until tender. Stir in carrots and tomatoes. Continue cooking about two minutes or until carrots are tender. Transfer mixture to bowl with chicken. Add cooked pasta and parmesan. Toss well.

Yield: 4 servings

CHICKEN RITZ

1   sleeve round buttery crackers, crushed
4-6 boneless, skinless, chicken breast halves
½   stick butter, melted
    favorite seasonings, lemon pepper, salt or garlic salt or onion salt, etc.

Dip chicken breasts in butter, sprinkle favorite seasonings, and roll in crushed crackers. Lay in a greased baking dish. Sprinkle any remaining crackers and butter over chicken pieces. Cover with foil. Bake at 350° for 40 minutes. Remove foil. Bake an additional ten minutes.

Yield: 4-6 servings

CHINESE CHICKEN HOW-SO

1   pound boneless, skinless chicken breasts
2   tablespoons butter or margarine
1   can golden mushroom soup
½   cup water
1   beef bouillon cube
1   tablespoon soy sauce
1   teaspoon Worcestershire sauce
½   teaspoon curry powder
½   teaspoon poppy seeds
1   (8-ounce) can bamboo shoots, drained
½   cup celery, sliced
½   cup onion, sliced
1   (3-ounce) can sliced mushrooms, drained
1   small green pepper, sliced into strips
3   tablespoons dry white wine
1   (3-ounce) can chow mein noodles

Cut chicken into 1 ½ inch pieces. Brown in butter until golden. Stir in soup, water, bouillon cube, soy sauce, Worcestershire sauce, curry and poppy seeds. Mix well. Cover and simmer about 15 minutes. Add bamboo shoots, celery, onion and mushrooms. Cover and simmer for ten minutes. Stir in green pepper and wine. Simmer three minutes more. Serve over chow mein noodles.

Yield: 4-6 servings

TERRY'S PECAN CHICKEN WITH JALAPENO BRIE SAUCE

4	boneless, skinless chicken breasts, pounded flat
1	cup pecans, processed to powder
2	cups flour
2	eggs
1	tablespoon milk
	salt to taste
	pepper to taste
	thyme to taste

Jalapeño Brie Sauce:

½	cup onions, diced
½	cup mushrooms, sliced
¼	cup jalapeños, canned or pickled
¼	cup butter
1	quart half and half
1	(4-ounce) package Brie cheese
	salt and white pepper to taste

In a bowl, mix together pecans, salt, pepper and thyme. (This breading will keep for a month in the refrigerator and also goes well with shrimp, fish and quail.) Mix eggs and milk in a small bowl. Dredge chicken breasts in flour, then in egg mixture and finally in pecan breading. The chicken may be deep fried in oil, or lightly browned on both sides in a saute´ pan with a little oil and baked at 350° for 20 minutes.

To make sauce, saute´ onions, muchrooms and jalapenos in butter until onions are translucent. Add in half and half, reserving one cup. Before mixture comes to a boil, add Brie cheese and watch constantly for burning on bottom of pan. Whisk until cheese is melted. Make a roux with three ounces melted butter and three ounces flour. Whisk to a smooth paste. Whisk the paste into the Brie mixture and bring to a boil so mixture thickens. Pour all into a blender and blend well. Strain through a cheese cloth. Using the reserved half and half, adjust consistency of sauce. Season to taste with salt and white pepper. To serve, ladle sauce over pecan breaded chicken.

Terry Kane - Owner and chef of Terry's Que Pasta. Terry's family has been in the active restaurant business since 1940, and he continues the tradition with his own very popular Terry's Que Pasta in Harlingen.

QUICK CHICKEN POT PIE

2 (9-inch) frozen pie shells, partially thawed
1 (10-ounce) can chicken, or cooked fresh chicken
1 can cream of chicken soup
1 (15-ounce) can mixed vegetables

Combine chicken, soup and vegetables. Pour into one pie shell. Invert other pie shell on top and pinch edges closed, using a fork. Bake at 350° for 45 minutes until brown.

This is an excellent way to use leftover chicken or turkey.

Yield: 4 servings

OLETA'S CHICKEN CASSEROLE

3 pounds boiled chicken breasts
1 can celery soup
1 can cream of chicken soup
1 cup sour cream
¾ cup celery, chopped and sauteed
⅓ cup ripe olives, chopped
1 package cornbread dressing
1 can chicken broth
½ stick margarine, melted

Cut chicken into bite sized pieces. Place in a 9 X 13-baking dish. Mix together celery soup, chicken soup, sour cream, celery, and olives. Spoon over chicken. Sprinkle dressing thoroughly over mixture. Combine chicken broth and margarine together. Pour over top of casserole. Bake at 350° for one hour.

Yield: 8-10 servings

HOT CHICKEN SALAD

2 cups chicken, diced (canned or fresh)
2 cups celery, chopped
2 tablespoons lemon juice
¼ cup onion, chopped
1 cup mayonnaise
salt and pepper to taste
plain potato chips

Mix together all ingredients except potato chips and pour into a 9 x 13-inch casserole dish. Top with crushed potato chips and bake at 350° for 20 minutes.

VEAL KNOTS PICCATA

2	pounds veal scallops, pounded thin
1	cup flour
½	teaspoon salt
¼	teaspoon white pepper
8	tablespoons butter
½	cup white wine
4	tablespoons fresh lemon juice
3	tablespoons capers, drained
2	egg yolks, beaten
4	tablespoons chopped parsley

Cut scallops into long strips, about one inch wide. Combine flour, salt and pepper. Roll veal strips in the dry mixture. Gently tie each strip into a knot. Re-season with the dry mixture, if necessary. Melt butter in a skillet and brown knots on all sides. Add wine, lemon juice and capers to meat. Simmer about six minutes or until tender. Remove meat from skillet to a warm serving platter. Make a sauce by adding egg yolks to the skillet. Blend quickly until thickened. Pour sauce over knots. Sprinkle with parsley to garnish.

CELEBRATION LAMB

1	(5-pound) leg of lamb
	salt to taste
	pepper to taste
	oregano to taste
	garlic cloves, peeled and sliced into fat slivers
¼	cup butter
	Juice of one large lemon
1	large onion, chopped
1	cup mushrooms, sliced
1	cup water

Translated on page 228

Place lamb, skin side up, in roasting pan. Rub with salt, pepper and oregano. Use tip of sharp knife to cut slits in lamb. Tuck in garlic slivers. Combine butter and lemon juice. Pour over meat. Add onions, mushrooms and half of water. Roast at 500° for 20 minutes. Add remaining water. Lower oven temperature to 350°. Roast until done. Baste occasionally.

Onions, mushroom and roasting juices are great served with rice.

Game
& Grilling

DUCK PATÉ

4	cups duck meat (4 boiled ducks)	
4	ounces mushrooms	
1	(8-ounce) package cream cheese	
5	ounces toasted almonds	
1	teaspoon Worcestershire sauce	
¼	teaspoon hot red pepper sauce	
1	teaspoon salt	
3	tablespoons onion, grated	
½	cup sour cream	
½	cup butter, melted	

Blend duck in a food processor. Process remaining ingredients. Add duck and blend well. Pour paté into desired container. Chill. Pour a thin coating of butter over the container to seal for freezing.

GAME PAELLA

	olive oil
1	large onion, chopped
4	cloves garlic, minced
	saffron to taste
2	cups long grain rice
1	(14-ounce) can peeled chopped tomatoes
4-6	quail breasts (1 per person - can substitute any game)
2	cups water
2	teaspoons salt
2	dozen black olives
½	pound venison or country sausage, sliced
1	(14-ounce) can artichoke hearts

Cover the bottom of a four quart dish or paella pan with olive oil and saute onions and garlic. Add saffron. Add raw rice and sauté two to three minutes. Add tomatoes and mix well. In a separate skillet, brown quail or game and season with salt and pepper. Place on top of rice mixture. Add water and salt. Arrange olives, venison or sausage and artichoke hearts around quail. Cover tightly with heavy foil. Bake at 400° for 50 to 60 minutes or over an open fire until rice is done.

Yield: 4-6 servings

GRILLED BASIL CHICKEN

¾   teaspoon pepper, coarsely ground
4   chicken breast halves, skinned
⅓   cup olive oil
¼   cup fresh basil, chopped
½   cup olive oil
2   tablespoons fresh basil, minced
1   tablespoon Parmesan cheese, grated
¼   teaspoon garlic powder
⅛   teaspoon salt
⅛   teaspoon pepper
    fresh basil sprigs (optional)

Gently press pepper into meaty sides of chicken breasts. Combine olive oil and basil. Stir well. Brush chicken lightly with mixture. Combine ½ cup olive oil, two tablespoons basil, Parmesan cheese, garlic powder, salt and pepper in a small bowl. Beat at low speed with an electric mixer until well blended and smooth. Transfer to a small serving bowl to be used for basting. Set aside. Grill chicken over medium coals for eight to ten minutes on each side. Baste frequently. Garnish with basil sprigs.

Yield: 4 servings

GRILLED HONEY CHICKEN

½   cup soy sauce
¼   cup sherry
¼   cup honey
1   garlic clove, crushed
¼   teaspoon ground ginger
3   teaspoons margarine, melted
2   (2 ½ pound) broiler fryers, cut in half

Combine first six ingredients. Cook five minutes, stirring constantly. Arrange chicken in a shallow pan. Cover with sauce and marinate fifteen minutes. Place chicken, skin side up, on the grill. Cook one hour, or until tender. Turn often and baste about every ten minutes.

Yield: 4 servings

BBQ CHICKEN

4	skinless, boneless chicken breast halves
¼	cup catsup
3	tablespoons cider vinegar
1	tablespoon white horseradish
1	teaspoon dark brown sugar
1	garlic clove, minced
⅛	teaspoon dried thyme
¼	teaspoon black pepper

To make sauce, combine catsup, vinegar, horseradish, brown sugar, garlic and thyme in a small saucepan. Mix well. Bring to a boil over medium-low heat. Cook, stirring frequently, about five minutes or until thickened. Remove from heat. Stir in pepper. Brush tops of chicken pieces lightly with sauce. Place chicken, sauce side down, on a foil lined grill rack or broiler pan. Brush other side lightly with sauce. Grill or broil, basting with remaining sauce and turning for five to seven minutes per side or until cooked.

Yield: 4 servings

MESQUITE GRILLED CHICKEN WITH TROPICAL BBQ SAUCE

½	cup BBQ sauce
¼	cup catalina-style salad dressing
3	ounces pineapple juice
1	teaspoon Italian seasoning
1	teaspoon poultry seasoning
¼	cup canola oil
6	skinless, boneless, chicken breast halves
	water-soaked mesquite wood chips

In a small bowl, combine first five ingredients to make the sauce. Add the canola oil after other ingredients are blended thoroughly. Heat gas grill and place wet mesquite chips on the briquettes. Baste chicken breasts on each side. Cook on medium heat, basting and turning frequently for about 20 minutes. The oil in the mixture will keep the sauce and chicken from burning.

Yield: 6 servings

QUAIL GRILLED IN CABBAGE LEAVES

½	cup butter or margarine
2	tablespoons snipped fresh parsley
¼	teaspoon dried thyme leaves
¼	teaspoon dried marjoram leaves
6	whole quail, skin on
6	large cabbage leaves
	salt

Melt butter in small saucepan. Stir in parsley, thyme and marjoram. Brush herb butter mixture over outside of birds. Wrap each bird with one leaf of cabbage, folding in the edges. Tie with wet kitchen string. Grill for fifteen minutes, turning frequently. Remove birds from grill. Carefully remove cabbage leaves and discard. Brush quail with remaining butter mixture. Grill birds until golden brown three to five minutes. Salt lightly before serving.

Yield: 4-6 servings

SOUTHERN QUAIL BREASTS

8	quail breasts
½	teaspoon salt
¼	teaspoon pepper
½	cup flour
½	cup butter, melted
½	cup mushrooms, chopped
½	cup onion, chopped
1	tablespoon parsley
½	cup white wine
½	cup whipping cream
	hot wild rice

Translated on page 223

Sprinkle quail with salt and pepper. Dredge in flour. In a large skillet, brown quail on both sides in butter. Remove quail. Sauté mushrooms, onions and parsley in pan drippings. Add quail and wine. Cover. Reduce heat to medium-low. Cook 30 minutes, basting frequently. Add whipping cream. Cook until thoroughly heated, but do not boil. Serve over wild rice.

Yield: 4 servings

TEXAS FRIED AND GRILLED QUAIL

8	whole quail
3	tablespoons honey
3	tablespoons balsamic vinegar
6	ounces jalapeño potato chips
½	cup dry breadcrumbs
	flour
2	eggs
	milk
	salt and pepper

Quarter the quail and marinate legs and thighs in honey and vinegar at least one hour. Remove bones and wings from breast sections. Grind potato chips and combine with breadcrumbs. Salt and pepper each breast and dust with flour. Beat eggs with a little milk. Dip floured breasts in egg and coat with crumbs. Refrigerate until ready to use. Grill or broil legs and fry the breasts in deep fry or skillet.

Yield: 4 servings

BBQ DOVES

12	doves
	milk
6	whole jalapeños, seeded and halved
	salt and pepper
6	slices bacon, halved
	Italian dressing

Marinate birds in milk overnight in the refrigerator. Remove from milk. Pat dry with paper towels. Put a piece of jalapeño inside cavity of each bird. Salt and pepper to taste. Wrap each with a half slice of bacon and secure with toothpick. Cook over a slow fire, basting frequently with dressing for about 30 minutes or until done.

Yield: 4 servings

CHARCOAL BROILED WHITEWINGS

Whitewing doves
bacon strips
jalapeño slices
garlic
onion slices
golden apple slices
butter or magarine
lemon

Cut the backbone out of the doves. Wash thoroughly then insert in the body cavity a slice of jalapeño, a slice of onion, a slice of apple. Wrap entire bird with a piece of bacon and hold together with toothpicks. Crush the garlic and sauté in the butter, then add lemon juice to make the basting sauce. Heat. Place the whitewings on a charcoal grill. Baste with the garlic-lemon-butter sauce and serve rare to medium rare.

It is essential to this dish that the whitewings or mourning doves be picked and not dressed. Most people will not believe that doves should be served rare, but once you have tasted them you will think you are eating the finest tenderloin.

Remember that the legs and thighs have one or two bites apiece and are a real delicacy if left on the bird. It is critical that the skin be left on the bird to keep the meat moist.

GRILLED GAME

doves, breasted and cleaned

1 fresh onion, cut into one inch
pieces

pickled jalapeño slices

8 ounces cream cheese, firm

thinly sliced bacon

Translated on page 223

On each dove breast, place one piece of onion and a jalapeño slice. Put one tablespoon slice of cream cheese on top. Wrap each dove breast with a bacon strip and secure with tooth-picks. Grill over low heat coals for ten to 20 minutes or until bacon is crisp. Follow this same procedure using pieces of venison. For variation, add a 1 x 1 chunk of Monterey Jack cheese.

DOVES AND DUMPLINGS

10-12 doves, picked and cleaned

½ cup flour

1 teaspoon salt

dash of pepper

3 tablespoons shortening or fat

2 cups water

Dumplings:

1 ½ cups flour, sifted

2 teaspoons baking powder

1 teaspoon salt

1 egg

½ cup milk

Roll birds in flour, salt and pepper. Brown well in hot fat in bottom of pressure cooker. Add water. Cover and cook at ten pounds pressure for 20 to 25 minutes, depending on size of birds. Reduce pressure normally. Remove birds and set aside. Reserve broth. To make the dumplings, sift flour with baking powder and salt. Beat egg. Add milk and combine with dry ingredients. Drop dumpling batter from spoon over meat broth. Simmer, uncovered for five minutes. Cover. Steam for five minutes. Remove dumplings to hot platter. Serve with birds. Use remaining broth for gravy.

Yield: 6 servings

ROAST DUCK

	pepper
2	ducks
1	orange
2	bacon strips
¼	cup white wine
1	tablespoon lemon juice
½	cup red currant jelly
1	tablespoon cornstarch dissoved in a small amount of water

Pepper ducks inside and out. Halve orange. Quarter and peel one half. Save other half for garnish. Stuff each duck with two orange quarters. Wrap each duck with a bacon strip. Place in a small roasting pan. Heat wine, lemon juice and jelly until jelly dissolves. Pour sauce over ducks. Roast at 400° for 25 minutes. Remove ducks to a heated platter. Skim fat off drippings and add cornstarch that has been blended with a small amount of water. Stir until sauce thickens. Pour over birds. Serve immediately.

SMOKED WILD TURKEY

1	wild turkey, preferably young
	salt
	pepper
1	(8-ounce) bottle creamy Italian dressing
¼	cup Worcestershire Sauce
¼	cup soy sauce
¼	cup lemon juice
3	teaspoons dry mustard

Salt and pepper inside and outside of turkey. Rub with Italian dressing and let marinate overnight. Mix remaining ingredients to make basting sauce. Place turkey on outdoor smoker and smoke one hour. Brush with basting sauce. Continue to smoke until tender, basting several times. Turkey will be done when leg moves easily.

SMOKED TURKEY MUSHROOM PECAN FETTUCINI

3	tablespoons unsalted butter
¼	cup onions, diced
3	tablespoons red bell pepper, dried
2	teaspoons garlic, minced
1	cup whipping cream
½	cup pecans, toasted and chopped
¼	cup smoked turkey (or chicken)
¼	cup ricotta cheese
2	tablespoons cilantro, minced
	8 ounces mushrooms, sliced
	10 to 12 ounces fettucine, cooked
	salt
	pepper

Melt butter over medium heat. Add onion, bell pepper and garlic and sauté until soft, about five minutes. Add whipping cream, pecans, turkey, ricotta cheese, cilantro and mushrooms and bring to boil, stirring continuously. Add pasta and cook over medium heat until warm. Season with salt and pepper.

Yield: 4 servings

SHRIMP EN BROCHETTE

3	dozen large raw shrimp, peeled, leaving tail attached
½	cup lemon juice
½	cup dry white wine
½	cup oil
¼	cup Worcestershire sauce
¼	cup soy sauce
	Monterey Jack cheese, sliced
	jalapeño peppers, sliced
	bacon, uncooked

Marinate shrimp for one hour or longer in lemon juice, wine, oil, Worcestershire Sauce and soy sauce. Slice shrimp down the back to the tail. Place a slice of Monterey jack cheese and jalapeño pepper inside shrimp and wrap with bacon. Skewer the prepared shrimp. Grill until shrimp and bacon are cooked. Baste with remaining marinade while cooking.

For a variation, substitute oysters for jalapenos and cheese. This marinade is also good to use with fresh vegetables that can be grilled at the same time (i.e. zucchini, squash, onions and mushrooms).

Yield: 6 servings

BACON WRAPPED SHRIMP

1	pound jumbo shrimp
6	slices bacon, uncooked
⅓	cup soy sauce
1	tablespoon cooking sherry
2	tablespoons garlic powder
	dash cayenne powder

Peel and devein shrimp. Cut bacon strips into thirds. Wrap bacon tightly around shrimp, securing with toothpick. Place in baking dish. Combine remaining ingredients and pour over shrimp, turning to coat well. Marinate for several hours in refrigerator. Broil each side under broiler for five minutes, until shrimp are pink and bacon is cooked through. Serve hot.

Yield: 16-20 appetizers

BARBECUE SHRIMP

1	pound jumbo shrimp
3	tablespoons cooking oil
2	tablespoons Pick-A Peppa sauce
2	tablespoons apricot preserves
1	tablespoon honey
1	tablespoon maple syrup
1	teaspoon red pepper
1	teaspoon peppercorns, crushed
¼	teaspoon basil, dried and crushed
¼	teaspoon oregano, dried and crushed
¼	teaspoon rosemary, dried and crushed
1	clove garlic, minced
1	pound bacon slices, uncooked
3	tablespoons lemon juice

Peel and devein shrimp. Combine all marinade ingredients, except for bacon and lemon juice, in a medium bowl. Add shrimp to the marinade and chill covered for one to six hours - the longer, the spicier. Partially cook bacon slices, making sure they are still limp. Cut bacon slices into halves and wrap around shrimp. Skewer shrimp and place on grill about four to five inches from heat. Brush lemon juice on shrimp. Cook over medium hot coals for eight to ten minutes, continuing to brush marinade on shrimp. Turn after four minutes. Serve over steamed zucchini with lemon wedges.

Yield: 4 servings

PICANTE GRILLED FISH

¾	cup low calorie Italian dressing
¾	cup picante sauce
2	pounds white fish fillets

Marinate fish in mixture of dressing and picante sauce. Remove from marinade and grill over hot coals or place under a broiler for 15 to 20 minutes. Cooking times vary. Do not overcook. Garnish with salsa, green onions, fresh tomatoes or cilantro.

Yield: 4 servings

GRILLED SALMON

½	cup butter
⅓	cup honey
⅓	cup brown sugar, packed
2	tablespoons lemon juice
1	(2-6 pound) salmon fillet, in one piece and skin on
1	teaspoon liquid smoke flavoring, optional

Combine butter, honey, brown sugar, lemon juice and liquid smoke in saucepan. Stir over medium heat for five to seven minutes. Mixture should be smooth. Salmon can be marinated in this mixture for thirty minutes or it can be used as a basting sauce when grilling. Lay foil on grill before warming. Lay salmon on foil with the skin on. Baste with mixture if not pre-marinated. Close cover of pit, cook forty-five minutes or until skin starts to flake off. Peel skin back, lemon to taste.

MARVELOUS LAMB

3 - 4 garlic cloves
1 onion, chopped
⅓ cup olive oil
 rind of two lemons, grated
½ cup lemon juice
 three inches or more of mint
1 teaspoon thyme
1 teaspoon rosemary
1 teaspoon tarragon
1 teaspoon marjoram
3 tablespoons brown sugar
2 teaspoons salt
2 teaspoons pepper
1 leg of lamb, butterflied

Sauté garlic and onion in olive oil about two minutes. Add remaining ingredients, except the lamb. Let simmer five minutes. Pour over lamb in shallow baking pan. Turn and marinate, basting every half hour for two to four hours. Insert meat thermometer into the thickest part of the lamb. Place lamb on charcoal grill that can be covered. Fire should be quite hot, but built to one side of grill only. Lamb should be placed opposite to, not on top of, charcoal. Cover and cook two and a half to three hours or until meat thermometer registers 175°. Baste frequently. During the last half hour, add two or three fistfuls of hickory chips on charcoal.

Yield: 6 large or 10 small servings

GRILLED PORK TENDERLOIN

1 (1 ½ - 2 pound) pork tenderloin
4-6 ounces Allegro marinade

Marinate pork 30 minutes to four hours. Cook over hot coals to desired doneness. Slice and serve. Great with chutney.

Yield: 4 servings

WILD PIG WITH MUSTARD SAUCE

3	tablespoons flour
2	tablespoons brown sugar
2	teaspoons dry mustard
2	teaspoons powdered thyme
1	teaspoon powdered sage
⅛	cup red wine vinegar
⅛	cup dry white wine
1	(5-pound) pig loin
4	cloves garlic, sliced
	salt and pepper to taste

Marinade:

1 ½	tablespoons flour
2	teaspoons powdered thyme
1	teaspoons powdered sage
¼	cup red wine vinegar
¼	cup dry white wine

Mix first five ingredients, then add vinegar and wine to make a paste. Puncture meat thoroughly and slip in slivers of garlic. Add salt and pepper to taste. Spread paste on meat. Place paste side down in a roaster. Spread remaining paste over the top of the meat. Place roaster in oven at 450° for ten to 12 minutes or until paste is crusty. Mix marinade ingredients and set aside. Turn oven down to 325°. Cover roaster. Cook an additional two and a half hours, basting often with the marinade. Remove meat. Skim fat from drippings and serve as gravy.

WILD PIG IN APPLE SCHNAPPS

1	(2 -3 pound) wild pig roast
¾	cup apple schnapps
2	tablespoons soy sauce
½	cup brown sugar
¼	cup apricot preserves
2	tablespoons oil
2	garlic cloves, crushed and minced
	salt and pepper

Using a little olive oil, brown pork thoroughly on all sides in a heavy skillet. Mix remaining ingredients. Put pork in baking dish. Pour schnapps mixture on top. Bake at 325° for one hour, basting every 20 minutes with pan drippings. If desired, thicken pan juices with one teaspoon cornstarch mixed with ½ cup water.

Yield: 6 servings

ROAST PORK IN BANANA LEAVES

5-6	pounds pork roast (or country ribs)
6-8	garlic cloves, minced
¾	cup oil
2	teaspoons salt
	banana leaves, washed

Mix garlic, oil and salt. Rub well into pork roast. Cover tightly with banana leaves. Tie with string like a package. Bake in a smoker for seven to nine hours or at 350° in an oven for 30 to 35 minutes per pound.

BIG TREE DEER CHILI

3	pounds venison, cubed
3	pounds pork sausage
2	teaspoons olive oil
2	teaspoons salt
2	teaspoons cumin
1	teaspoon pepper
⅛	teaspoon cayenne pepper
4-6	tablespoons chili powder
1	(8-ounce) can tomato sauce
2	cups water
1	teaspoon garlic powder
2	tablespoons cornmeal
1	tablespoon flour
1	cup water

In a large pot, brown the meat in oil. Drain. Add salt, cumin, pepper, cayenne pepper, chili powder, tomato sauce, water and garlic powder to meat and bring to a boil. Make a paste with cornmeal, flour and water and add to chili. Cook slowly for three hours, stirring often.

Translated on page 222

HUNGRY HUNTER'S VENISON STEW

1 ½   pounds venison, cut into
       ½-inch cubes
½   pound smoked sausage, cut
       into ½ inch slices
2   tablespoons vegetable oil
½   cup onion, chopped
½   cup celery, chopped
2   (28-ounce) cans tomatoes,
       undrained and chopped
1   (12-ounce) can beer
1   tablespoon salt
1   tablespoon sugar
½   tablespoon ground pepper
2   carrots, diced
2   medium potatoes, cubed

Brown venison and sausage in hot oil in large pot. Add onions and celery. Cook until tender. Add tomatoes, beer, salt, sugar, ground pepper and carrots. Cover and cook 30 minutes. Add potatoes and cook additional 30 minutes or until done.

Yield: 2 quarts

QUICK VENISON ROTINI SOUP

1   pound ground venison
1   (6-ounce) can whole tomatoes,
       cut up and juice reserved
1   (8-ounce) can tomato sauce
2   envelopes chili seasoning mix
4   cups water
1 ½   cups uncooked rotini noodles
1   (10-ounce) package frozen
       mixed vegetables
1   tablespoon sugar
1   tablespoon minced onion
1   cup sour cream
1   tablespoon driedchives

In dutch oven, brown meat over medium heat, stirring occasionally. Drain if necessary. Stir in tomatoes and juice, tomato sauce and chili seasoning mix. Add water, rotini, vegetables, onion and sugar, mix well. Heat to boiling. Cover and reduce heat. Simmer ten to 15 minutes or until rotini is tender. Various types of game can be substituted.

In small dish, mix sour cream and chives. Serve with soup as garnish.

GRETCHEN'S NILGAI MEAT SAUCE

2	pounds ground nilgai
1	large onion, chopped
6-8	garlic cloves, chopped
3	stalks celery and leaves, chopped
2	(12-ounce) cans tomato paste
1	(14-ounce) can tomatoes, undrained and mashed
1	tablespoon sugar
3	tablespoons Italian dressing
1	small green pepper, chopped
1	cup mushrooms, sliced
1	cup green or black olives (or both)
1	teaspoon black pepper
1	teaspoon garlic salt
2	teaspoons salt
½	teaspoon dried red chili flakes
½	cup white wine
4	cups water

Brown nilgai in large eight quart pot. Add onion, green pepper, celery, and garlic and stir to mix. Add mushrooms, tomato paste, tomatoes, olives, sugar, italian dressing, pepper, salt, red chili and garlic salt and stir to mix. Add wine and water. Cover and simmer for one hour.

GROUND VENISON MEAT SAUCE

6	pounds ground venison or other game animal
6	tablespoons bacon drippings
6	medium onions, chopped
3	jalapeños, chopped
2	packages taco mix
2	packages chili mix
1	(28-ounce) can chopped tomatoes
1	(20-ounce) jar picante sauce
2	cans beef broth

Brown meat in an eight quart pot with six tablespoons of bacon drippings. In skillet, saute onions and add to pot with all remaining ingredients. Simmer three to four hours. Add water as necessary.

This recipe makes a ton of meat sauce and is great for a party. Can be used for lasagne, tacos or chili!!

COUNTRY FRIED VENISON TENDERLOIN

1	venison tenderloin	
1	egg	
1	cup milk	
1	sleeve round buttery crackers, crushed	
	salt	
	pepper	
½	cup flour	
	vegetable oil	

Slice tenderloin thinly, approximately ¼ to ½ inch. Gently pound each slice to tenderize. Mix egg and milk in bowl. In another bowl, mix crackers, salt, pepper and flour. Dredge tenderloin in egg mixture, then roll in crumb mixture. In skillet with a little oil, pan fry on medium high heat. Cook about two minutes and turn, cooking one more minute. Do not over cook. Change oil often.

BIG GAME BAKED ROUND STEAKS

2-3	pounds boneless elk, antelope or venison
½	cup flour
	salt
	pepper
2	tablespoons butter
2-3	tablespoons olive or vegetable oil
3	tablespoons onion, chopped
1	teaspoon brown sugar
1	teaspoon catsup
	dried basil leaves
¼	cup beef broth

Cut meat into 1-inch thick serving pieces. Gently pound meat to ½-inch thickness. Season with salt and pepper on both sides. Dip steak in flour, both sides. In large skillet, melt butter and oil over medium high heat. Brown meat. Add additional oil if necessary. Arrange steaks in 12 x 18-baking pan. Sprinkle steaks with onion, top with brown sugar and catsup. Dot with butter. Add beef broth to skillet and cook one minute to loosen any browned bits. Pour broth to baking pan and cover with foil. Bake at 350° for 30 to 45 minutes. Add additional water during cooking if meat appears dry.

VENISON BACKSTRAP AND MUSHROOMS

4	tablespoons butter
2	tablespoons vegetable oil
1 ½	pounds sliced venison backstrap
5-7	large mushrooms
4	green onions, chopped
½	cup cooking wine
½	can beef consomme
	pepper

In skillet, heat butter and oil. Cook meat four to five minutes. Add mushrooms and onions. Season with pepper and cook about four to five minutes longer. While cooking, add wine and consomme. Turn heat down and cover. Simmer on low for one to one and a half hours. Serve over rice.

VENISON GUISADA

¼	cup oil
1	pound venison backstrap, cut into chunks
2	tablespoons flour
½	cup water
1	can tomatoes, diced or mashed, juice reserved
1	clove garlic, minced
2	teaspoons cumin
	pepper
	salt, if desired

Brown venison in oil. Remove from pan. Add flour and water to pan drippings to make a thick gravy. If necessary, thin with juice from the tomatoes and more water. Add meat, tomatoes, garlic, cumin, and pepper to gravy mixture. Simmer until meat is tender. Serve alone, over rice or with flour tortillas.

VENISON MARSALA

venison backstrap or tenderloin medallions, cut approx. ¼ inch thick

flour

salt and pepper

olive oil

1 yellow onion

mushrooms

2-4 garlic cloves, crushed or minced

¼ cup white wine, either chablis or chardonnay

½ cup marsala (sweet Italian cooking wine)

Lay tenderloin or backstrap medallions on a cutting board, pound lightly with a meat mallet on both sides until slightly flattened. Add salt and pepper to flour and dredge venison in flour. Set aside. Heat olive oil in a frying pan. Add onion, mushrooms and garlic to olive oil. Sauté until onion and garlic bits are clear but not brown. Drain onion and garlic and reserve oil. Place pan back over fire and add white wine to skillet (deglaze). Be prepared for white wine to sizzle and steam. Scrape up any bits of onion or garlic left in bottom of pan, then pour wine over onion, garlic and mushrooms and let stand. Pour reserved olive oil back into pan, sauté venison pieces a few at a time, cooking on each side. As they begin to brown, remove to a warm plate and keep in warm oven until remaining pieces of venison are cooked. When all venison has been cooked, pour off olive oil and add marsala to skillet, scraping up remainder of any venison or flour left in bottom. Add onion, garlic and mushrooms with white wine to marsala. Allow marsala to reduce slightly, then pour over venison pieces and serve.

OLD FASHIONED VENISON ROAST

1	(3 - 5 pound) venison roast or ham
1	bunch celery
2	cans French onion soup
1	teaspoon garlic powder
½	teaspoon marjoram
½	teaspoon thyme
½	teaspoon black pepper
2	cans water
	salt to taste

Layer celery stalks to cover bottom of a large roasting pan. Wash and trim waste from venison. Add soup, spices, water and meat to roasting pan. Bring to a boil; reduce heat to simmer. Cover and simmer four to five hours, turning roast occasionally, until done. This may also be cooked in a covered dish in the oven at 325° for one hour, then reduce to 250° for four hours. Discard celery before serving.

STUFFED VENISON ROAST

1	(5-pound) venison roast
1	venison tenderloin, browned
8	ounces milk
2	white rolls, diced
8	ounces venison or veal meat
4	ounces mushrooms
2	eggs
3	ounces herbs, freshly chopped
½	red bell pepper, diced
½	onion, diced
½	package spinach, blanched
4	slices bacon
4	ounces pecans, chopped

To make stuffing, heat milk and pour over diced rolls. Let soak for five minutes and set rolls aside. Grind venison or veal. Add mushrooms, eggs, chopped herbs, bell pepper and onion. Mix with rolls and refrigerate.

Take venison roast and split sideways to butterfly. Spread stuffing evenly over meat, cover with blanched spinach and put roasted venison tenderloin in the middle. Roll up roast and sew up end with strings. Roll roast in pecans and bake at 350° for one and one half hours.

STEAK KABOBS

2	tablespoons soy sauce	In a shallow glass dish, combine soy sauce, honey, ginger, garlic, lemon peel, and red pepper flakes. Mix well. Add beef and stir to coat. Cover with plastic wrap and refrigerate one to two hours, stirring occasionally. Start grill or preheat broiler. Remove beef from marinade. Discard marinade. Using four 10-inch metal skewers, alternately thread beef, tomatoes, mushroom and bell pepper. Place on grill or broiler two inches from the heat. Cook about ten minutes, turning often, until meat is medium-rare and vegetables are lightly brown. Serve immediately.
2	tablespoons honey	
1	teaspoon ground ginger	
1	garlic clove, crushed	
1	teaspoon lemon peel, grated	
¼	teaspoon crushed red pepper flakes	
12	ounces boneless sirloin, trimmed and cut into one inch cubes	
8	cherry tomatoes	
8	medium mushrooms	
1	green bell pepper, cored, seeded and cut into eight squares	
1	large white onion, cut into squares	

Yield: 4 Servings

At the final close of the Harlingen Air Force Base in the 1960's, grocery store founder H.E. Butt purchased the base jail building and donated it to the city to be used as a museum. Over the years, the Rio Grande Valley Museum has added a number of historically significant buildings to its complex, including the home of Harlingen's founder, Lon C. Hill, and Harlingen's first hospital (complete with physician's office, equipment, surgical suite and pharmacy). Also included in the museum's "collection" is the Paso Real, moved from the banks of the arroyo, where it served as an early stagecoach rest stop and "hotel."

INDONESIAN BEEF SKEWERS

1 ½   pounds lean boneless beef
      sirloin (chicken or pork)
1   garlic clove, minced or pressed
2   tablespoons soy sauce
1   tablespoon salad oil
1   teaspoon ground cumin
1   teaspoon coriander

Peanut Sauce:
1   cup water
⅔   cup creamy peanut butter
2   garlic cloves, minced or pressed
2   tablespoons brown sugar
1 ½   tablespoons lemon juice
1   tablespoon soy sauce
⅓   teaspoon crushed red pepper

Translated on page 224

Cut beef into one inch cubes. In a bowl, combine garlic, soy sauce, oil, cumin and coriander. Add beef and stir to coat. Cover and refrigerate at least two hours or until the next day, stirring occasionally. Prepare 10-12 long bamboo skewers by soaking in hot water at least 30 minutes or until the next day. Lift meat from marinade and drain briefly. Thread four or five pieces of meat on each skewer. Arrange skewers on a lightly greased grill two to four inches above a solid bed of hot coals. Cook, turning often, until well browned, (eight to ten minutes for medium-rare). To make peanut sauce, combine water, peanut butter and garlic in a two quart pan. Cook over medium to low heat, stirring, until mixture boils and thickens. Remove from heat and stir in brown sugar, lemon juice, soy and pepper. Serve with hot meat skewers.

Yield: 4 - 6 Servings

ESSIE'S BBQ SAUCE

3   cloves garlic
      Juice of one lemon
2   teaspoons hickory smoked salt
2   (14-ounce) bottles catsup
1   small jar French's mustard
2   (5-ounce) bottles
      Worcestershire sauce
1   cup vegetable oil
1-3   jalapeños

Pulverize garlic in press. Add lemon juice, salt, pepper, catsup and mustard. Stir well. Add Worcestershire sauce and oil. Whip or beat with a mixer. Add jalapeños to your taste.

For a variety, use smoky flavored worcestershire instead of flavored salt.

SHISH-KA-BOB MARINADE

1	small jar Italian dressing
½	cup tomato/clam juice
2	tablespoons soy sauce
⅓	cup Pick-a-Peppa sauce
1	teaspoon Worcestershire sauce
½	teaspoon red pepper
½	cup green pepper, finely diced
1	small onion, finely diced
	salt to taste

Combine all ingredients. Use to baste venison or other game on the grill.

LEMON-GARLIC GRILLING SAUCE

½	cup butter or margarine, melted
½	teaspoon hot pepper sauce
¼	cup lemon juice
1	tablespoon Worcestershire sauce
1-3	garlic cloves, peeled and minced
¼	teaspoon black pepper

In a small bowl, combine all ingredients until well blended. Brush on seafood, poultry or vegetables during grilling or broiling. Heat any remaining sauce and serve with grilled foods. Makes ¾ cup.

PICANTE GAME MARINADE

3	cups picante sauce
6	tablespoons brown sugar
1	teaspoon garlic powder
2	tablespoons spicy mustard
2	tablespoons soy sauce
1	teaspoon liquid smoke

Blend all ingredients in a mixing bowl. Pour into a blender and pulse until smooth. Use as a marinade or basting sauce for any wild game or cornish hens.

Yield: 8 servings

ONION RELISH

3	red onions
1	serrano pepper, chopped
3-4	sprigs cilantro, chopped
2	teaspoons cider vinegar or
	juice of ½ lemon
	salt

Slice onions into very thin rings. Separate the onion rings. Wash in several changes of cold water. Drain, squeezing gently so as not to bruise the onion rings. Place in non-metallic bowl and toss with serrano and cilantro, vinegar (or lemon juice), and salt to taste.

Yield: 6-8 servings

BUTTER ROASTED CORN

6	tablespoons butter
1 ½	teaspoons garlic salt
3	tablespoons parsley, minced
	dash paprika
6	large ears corn or
	12 small ears corn

Combine butter and garlic salt. Spread on corn. Sprinkle with parsley and paprika. Tightly seal each ear in foil. Grill over hot coals 15 minutes, turning frequently. Partially unwrap and serve in foil.

Yield: 6 servings

GRILLED BAKED POTATOES

4	whole potatoes
½	cup butter
1	purple onion

Wash potatoes and slice ¼ inch thick ¾ of the way through the potato. Place a slice of butter and a slice of onion in each cut. Wrap in foil. Set in hot charcoals of grill and bake for 45 minutes to one hour.

Yield: 4 servings

GRILLED ROSEMARY NEW POTATOES

4   large new potatoes or
     6 medium new potatoes
¼   cup olive oil
     garlic salt
     pepper
     rosemary, dry or freshly chopped

Cut potatoes into ½ inch cubes and place on skewers. Brush with olive oil. Sprinkle with garlic salt, pepper and rosemary. Drizzle again with olive oil. Place skewers on grill for 45 minutes to one hour, until golden.

Yield: 4 servings

STUFFED 1015 ONIONS

4   large 1015 sweet onions
     salt to taste
1   pound ground venison, cooked
     and drained
1   envelope mushroom gravy mix
½   cup soft breadcrumbs
¼   cup milk
1   egg, lightly beaten
¼   teaspoon ground sage
¼   teaspoon black pepper
¼   cup fresh parsley, chopped

Peel onions and cut into halves. Remove the centers and set the shells aside. Chop the center and mix with the remaining ingredients (except parsley). Spoon mixture into onion shells and wrap in foil. Seal lightly. Grill 35 to 40 minutes over medium coals. Garnish with parsley before serving.

Translated on page 222

Great Kiskadee, greenjay, groove-billed ani, chachalaca...these are some of the 450-plus reasons the Rio Grande Valley is the number one bird-watching area in Texas, and Texas is the number one bird-watching destination in the U.S. 468 bird species have been sighted in the Valley with 34 of these regular occurring species found nowhere else in the country. In 1994, Harlingen paid tribute to its colorful wealth of rare birds species by founding the Rio Grande Valley Birding Festival, a multi-day event that attracts thousands of eco-tourists.

CANTALOUPE SALSA

½   large cantaloupe
¾   cup red bell pepper, finely diced
¼   cup cilantro, finely chopped
3   tablespoons green onion, finely
    chopped
    juice of one lime
    pinch of salt
    pinch of dried hot pepper flakes

Remove the seeds and rind from the cantaloupe. Chop into a very fine dice. Put in a glass bowl. Stir together the red bell pepper, cilantro, green onions, and lime juice. Add the salt and hot pepper flakes. Chill well before serving.

Serve over grilled chicken breasts or fish. Any other firm fruit can be substituted.

CRANBERRY SALSA

1   cup cranberries
    Juice of ½ orange
⅓   cup sugar
3   medium serrano or jalapeño
    peppers, peeled, seeded and
    minced
3   tablespoons cilantro, chopped
2   tablespoons pecans, toasted
    Zest of ½ lime
    Zest of ½ orange
    salt to taste

In a food processor, blend cranberries, orange juice and sugar for 30 to 45 seconds. Transfer to a mixing bowl and add remaining ingredients. Let sit for at least 30 minutes before serving.

This salsa is the perfect accompaniment for wild game, especially wild pig. It also serves as a zippy alternative to cranberry sauce at the traditional Thanksgiving dinner!!

Monica Burdette - Inn at El Canelo. Tucked away in the rugged ranch country north of Raymondville, this bed and breakfast offers a relaxing get away as well as private dinner parties.

Seafood

CAPER SAUCE FOR SEAFOOD

1   cup fresh parsley, chopped
¼   cup green onion, chopped
1   garlic clove, finely chopped
2   tablespoons capers
⅔   cup mayonnaise
2   tablespoons oil
1   tablespoon lemon juice
½   teaspoon mustard

Combine parsley, green onions and garlic in food processor until pureed. Add remaining ingredients and blend well. Chill.

Yield: 1 ½ cup

PAPAYA SALSA

2   ripe papayas (about 1 pound each)
½   cup purple onion, finely chopped
1   red or green jalapeño pepper, seeded, finely chopped
1   large garlic clove, finely minced
¼   cup fresh cilantro, chopped
½   cup fresh lime juice
   zest of two limes, shredded

Toss all ingredients together. Serve with fish.

Yield: 4 cups

SWEET PEPPER SAUCE FOR FISH

1   pint green tomatoes, ground (no juice)
2   red sweet peppers, ground
2   green sweet peppers, ground
1   teaspoon salt
6   sweet pickles, ground
1   cup sugar
2   tablespoons flour
2   tablespoons prepared mustard
½   cup vinegar
1   cup sour cream
3   eggs, beaten

Mix tomatoes, peppers and salt. Let stand a few minutes and drain. Add sweet pickles. Mix sugar, flour, mustard, vinegar, sour cream and eggs. Bring to a boil. Pour over tomato mixture. Mix well. Pour into jars and seal.

SEAFOOD MARINADE

1 cup vegetable oil
1 cup lemon or lime juice
2 teaspoons Italian salad
   dressing mix
2 tablespoons light soy sauce
¼ cup brown sugar
⅓ cup green onions, chopped
1 teaspoon salt
¼ teaspoon cajun seasoning
   garlic, minced to taste
   fresh ginger, shredded, to taste

Combine all ingredients and marinate seafood three to four hours. Grill or broil seafood. Use sauce for basting during grilling.

SEAFOOD PASTA SALAD

1 (12-ounce) package vermicelli
5 hard cooked eggs, chopped
5 celery ribs, chopped
6 tablespoons sweet pickle relish
3 tablespoons yellow onion, minced
1 ½ tablespoons mayonnaise
   (no substitute)
1 cup shrimp or crab, freshly
   cooked and cleaned
   paprika

Prepare vermicelli according to directions on package. Drain, rinse, and let cool. Mix next six ingredients with pasta and chill. Toss lightly with crab or shrimp before serving. Sprinkle with paprika for color. Chopped green peppers or black olives can be added for variety.

Yield: 10 servings

1	tablespoon olive oil
1	red bell pepper, seeded and julienned
1	medium onion, sliced
½	teaspoon dried basil
½	teaspoon dried thyme
½	teaspoon dried oregano
1	bayleaf, crumbled
1	(16-ounce) can chopped tomatoes, drained (reserve 1 cup of liquid)
3	garlic cloves, minced
1	(9-ounce) package frozen artichoke hearts
1 ½	cups raw shrimp, shelled and deveined
1 ½	cups raw bay scallops
1	cup quick cooking rice, uncooked

Translated on page 215

Heat oil in skillet until hot. Add red pepper, onion, herbs, tomatoes and garlic. Cover and cook about five minutes, stirring occasionally. Add artichoke hearts and cook five more minutes. Add tomato juice and seafood. Bring to a boil and stir in uncooked rice. Return to a boil. Remove from heat and let stand, covered, for eight to ten minutes. Serve immediately.

Yield: 4 servings

Golden-fronted Woodpecker

ELEGANT SEAFOOD LASAGNA

8	lasagna noodles, cooked al dente
1	cup green onions, chopped
2	tablespoons butter
1	(8-ounce) package cream cheese, softened
1 ½	cups cottage cheese
1	egg
2	teaspoons basil
½	teaspoon salt
	dash of pepper
2	(10 1/2-ounce) cans cream of mushroom soup
⅓	cup milk
⅓	cup white wine
1	pound boiled shrimp, peeled
2	(6 1/2-ounce) cans crabmeat
1	cup Mozzarella cheese, shredded
⅓	cup Parmesan cheese, shredded
½	cup sharp Cheddar cheese, shredded

Sauté onions in butter. In a blender or food processor, blend buttered onions, cream cheese, cottage cheese, egg, basil, salt and pepper. In a separate bowl, mix together the soup, milk, wine, shrimp and crabmeat. Layer as follows: Place four cooked noodles in the bottom of a greased pan. Spoon over ½ of cream cheese mixture and then ½ of seafood mixture. Repeat layers. Add Mozzarella cheese on top and sprinkle with Parmesen cheese. Bake at 350° for 45 minutes. After removing from the oven, top with Cheddar cheese and let set for ten minutes.

Yield: 10 servings

Translated on page 218

With the coming of affordable air transportation, life in the Rio Grande Valley changed radically. No longer faced with a 300 mile drive that crossed the 90 mile lonely stretch of the King Ranch, locals could now venture forth on weekend excursions to the bright lights of big cities of the state and beyond. Hordes of visitors seeking to take advantage of the white sands of South Padre Island, the proximity to Mexico, the hunter's paradise and the wildlife sanctuaries began to pour into our area. The beautiful Valley International Airport is the center of this busy airline traffic and is served by Southwest Airlines, American, and Continental.

CAMARONES ENCHILADOS
(Shrimp Enchilado)

1 ¼   pounds medium raw shrimp,
     peeled and de-veined
½   cup olive oil
1   medium onion, sliced thin
3   garlic cloves, minced
1   medium-large green pepper,
     sliced into ¼ inch strips
½   cup parsley, finely minced
1   (4-ounce) jar pimiento, undrained
1   (8-ounce) can tomato sauce
½   cup catsup
½   cup dry white wine
1   teaspoon white vinegar
1   large bay leaf
1 ½   teaspoons salt
1   teaspoon of seasoned salt
     flavor enhancer
1   teaspoon ground black pepper
1   teaspoon Worcestershire sauce
1   teaspoon hot pepper sauce

In a large skillet, heat the oil. Add shrimp, and cook stirring frequently until shrimp are partially opaque and pink. Do not cook through. Remove shrimp with a slotted spoon and set aside in a bowl. To the oil in the skillet, add onions, garlic and green pepper and saute on medium heat until onions are translucent, stirring frequently. Add parsley, pimientos and their liquid and stir to blend well. Add remaining ingredients. Stir well, lower heat to medium-low and cook slowly for 20 - 25 minutes. Add shrimp and any liquid which may be in the bowl, stir well, and cook an additional three to five minutes or until the shrimp are just cooked through. Can be made a day ahead and reheated, but be careful not to overcook shrimp.

Despite the name, the orgin of this dish is Spanish, not Mexican, and is actually a Cuban recipe. This dish is versatile in that it is designed to be served as a dinner entree over white rice! Serve with a green salad and hot french bread.

Yield: 4 - 6 servings

JAMBALAYA

1	tablespoon bacon fat
2	medium onions, chopped
2	packages spicy link sausage, sliced
1	tablespoon flour
2	cups ham, diced
1	(16-ounce) can whole tomatoes, drained and chopped
1	cup rice, uncooked
1	large garlic clove, minced
2	cups chicken broth
¼	teaspoon of cayenne pepper (or more, to taste)
½	teaspoon dried thyme
1	medium green bell pepper, diced
3	tablespoons parsley, minced
2	pounds raw shrimp, shelled

Melt bacon fat in a heavy pot with tight fitting lid. Add onions and sausage. Cook over medium heat, stirring often, until sausage is slightly browned and onions are translucent. Add flour and cook slowly, stirring constantly, until mixture turns light brown. Add ham and tomatoes. Cover tightly and simmer over low heat for about 30 minutes. Add rice, garlic, chicken broth, seasonings, bell pepper and parsley. Cover tightly and simmer another 40 minutes or until the rice is cooked, but not mushy. Do not stir. Add shrimp and stir until well distributed in the pot. Cook on low for five minutes. Season to taste.

Yield: 6 - 8 servings

SPAGHETTI PROVENCAL

1	large shallot, minced
1	large tomato, seeded, skinned and diced
2	tablespoons parsely, chopped
1	tablespoon white wine vinegar
¼	cup olive oil
6-8	raw scallops
6-8	raw shrimp
2	tablespoons olive oil
1	(12-ounce) package spaghetti, cooked al dente

Translated on page 214

Combine shallots, tomato, parsley, wine vinegar and olive oil in a medium saucepan. Bring to a boil, reduce heat and simmer for about two minutes. In a large skillet, saute shrimp and scallops in two tablespoons olive oil over medium heat. Cook until shrimp turn pink and scallops turn opaque. Add seafood to tomato sauce and mix well. Serve over spaghetti and serve at once.

Yield: 4 servings

SHRIMP RICE CASSEROLE

2	cups soft bread crumbs
6	tablespoons butter, melted
1	tablespoon onion, minced
3	tablespoons flour
1 ½	teaspoons curry powder
1	teaspoons salt
⅛	teaspoon cayenne pepper
2 ¼	cups milk
2	cups rice, cooked
1	cup peas, cooked
2	cups cooked shrimp, peeled

Toss bread crumbs in three table-spoons melted butter. Set aside. Cook onion in remaining butter until tender. Stir in flour, curry, salt and cayenne pepper. Gradually add milk. Cook over low heat until thickened. Fold in rice, peas and shrimp. Pour into 2-quart casserole dish. Top with bread crumbs. Bake at 350° for 20 minutes. One can of quartered artichoke hearts may be added for variety.

Yield: 6 servings

SEAFOOD WILD RICE CASSEROLE

1	(6-ounce) package brown wild rice
1	pound fresh or frozen crab meat
1	pound cooked shrimp, peeled
3	(10 ½-ounce) cans mushroom soup, undiluted
⅓	cup onion, chopped
1	cup green pepper, chopped
1	cup celery, chopped
2	cups fresh mushrooms, sliced

Prepare rice according to package instructions. Add all remaining ingredients and mix well. Spoon into light-ly greased four quart casserole. Bake uncovered at 325° for one hour.

Yield: 6 servings

UNCLE JOE'S EASY SHRIMP ETOUFEE

⅓   cup cooking oil
⅓   cup all-purpose flour
1 ½   onion, chopped
1   cup celery, chopped
½   cup bell pepper, chopped
3   garlic cloves, minced
⅓   cup water
½   cup green onion tops, chopped
2   tablespoons parsley, snipped
1   tablespoon lemon juice
1   teaspoon cayenne pepper
1   tablespoon black pepper
1   pound raw shrimp, peeled
      and deveined

To prepare roux, combine oil and flour in a large saucepan. Stir constantly over medium low heat until brown, approximately ten minutes. Add onion, celery, bell pepper and garlic and cook 20 minutes, stirring occasionally. Add water, green onion, parsley, lemon juice, black pepper and cayenne pepper. Simmer for 30 minutes on low heat. Add shrimp and simmer five to eight minutes until shrimp is pink. Serve over hot cooked white rice. Sprinkle with file' if desired.

Yield: 6 servings

MY DADDY'S SHRIMP CREOLE

3   tablespoons oil
1   onion, chopped
1   bell pepper, chopped
1   cup celery, chopped
1   (28-ounce) can whole tomatoes,
      chopped
1   (8-ounce) can tomato sauce
½   teaspoon pepper
1   teaspoon salt
¼   teaspoon cayenne pepper
      (optional)
1   pound raw shrimp, peeled
      and de-veined

Combine oil, onion, bell pepper and celery in a large skillet and saute until celery is tender. Add chopped tomatoes and tomato sauce, pepper, salt and cayenne pepper. Bring to a boil and reduce heat. Add shrimp and cook until shrimp are pink, about five minutes. Do not over cook shrimp. The oil can be reduced or even omitted if you use a reduced calorie spray.

Yield: 6-8 servings

EASY SHRIMP SCAMPI

1 ½   pounds large or extra large
      shrimp, cooked and peeled
2   sticks butter
2   teaspoons garlic powder
      (not garlic salt)
2   tablespoons spicy mustard
½   teaspoon red pepper flakes

In microwave, melt butter and add remaining ingredients. Place shrimp in bowls that can go in microwave. Pour sauce over shrimp and microwave until sizzling. Sprinkle with parsley.

Yield: 4 servings

SHRIMP SCAMPI

1   pound raw large shrimp,
      peeled and deveined
6   garlic cloves, finely chopped
¼   cup dry white wine
¼   cup olive oil
¼   cup butter, melted
3   tablespoons parsley

Mix garlic, wine, oil, butter and parsley in small bowl. Arrange shrimp in baking dish and pour mixture on top. Toss to coat. Place under broiler and cook approximately five minutes, turning occassionally until shrimp turns pink. Serve over white and wild rice or linguini.

Yield: 4 servings

SPICY BAKED SHRIMP

½   cup olive oil
2   tablespoons cajun or creole
      seasoning
2   tablespoons fresh lemon juice
2   tablespoons parsley, finely
      chopped
1   tablespoon honey
1   tablespoon soy sauce
      pinch of cayenne pepper
1   pound large raw shrimp,
      shelled and de-veined

Combine first seven ingredients in a 9x13-inch baking dish. Add shrimp and toss to coat. Refrigerate one hour. Bake at 450°, stirring occasionally, until shrimp are pink and cooked through. Garnish with lemon wedges and serve with plenty of French bread.

Yield: 4 servings

SHRIMP SICILY ALFREDO

1 ½   pounds large shrimp,
       peeled and deveined
¼   cup flour
       salt and pepper
3   tablespoons butter or margarine,
       melted
3   tablespoons olive oil
2   large garlic cloves, minced
2   teaspoons dried oregano
2   tablespoons parsley, chopped
       juice of one large lemon

Pat shrimp dry on paper towels. In a small bowl, season flour with salt and pepper. In a large skillet, heat butter and oil with garlic and oregano over medium high heat. Lightly flour shrimp, then quickly stir-fry in hot oil, reducing heat as necessary. Shrimp should begin to become firm and turn pink in four to five minutes depending on their size. Immediately before removing shrimp from skillet, stir in parsley and lemon juice. Serve with Fettuccine Alfredo.

Fettuccine Alfredo:
½   pound fettucini
⅓   cup butter, softened
¾   cup whipping cream
¾   cup Parmesan cheese, shredded
½   teaspoon salt
⅛   teaspoon white pepper
       dash ground nutmeg
       course ground pepper

In dutch oven, prepare fettucini according to package directions; drain. Remove pan from heat. In the same pan, combine fettucini and butter; toss to coat. Add one half of the cream; toss well. Add one half of the Parmesan; toss well. Add remaining cream; toss well. Add remaining cheese and seasonings; toss well until coated and creamy. Arrange in a warm serving dish. Serve immediately with Shrimp Sicily.

Yield: 4 servings

NEW ORLEANS STYLE SHRIMP

1	stick butter
1 ½	teaspoons minced garlic
1	teaspoon Worcestershire sauce
1	teaspoon black pepper
1	teaspoon cayenne pepper
½	teaspoon salt
½	teaspoon crushed red pepper
½	teaspoon dry thyme leaves, crushed
½	teaspoon rosemary leaves, crushed
⅛	teaspoon oregano
1	pound medium raw shrimp, peeled and deveined
5	tablespoons butter
½	cup shrimp stock
¼	cup beer at room temperature

In 12-inch sauté pan, melt one stick butter with garlic, Worcestershire sauce and next seven ingredients (spices). When butter is melted, add shrimp. Cook uncovered on medium high heat for two minutes, shaking, not stirring. Add five tablespoons butter and shrimp stock, cook and shake two minutes. Add beer, cook one more minute. Serve immediately.
Yield: 4 servings

Translated on page 217

DRUNKEN SHRIMP ON PASTA

1	(12-ounce) package fettucini
3	tablespoons butter
24	large raw shrimp, peeled and deveined
	salt
	freshly ground pepper
2	jalapeños, sliced and seeded (can use red and green)
½	cup green onion, chopped
	Zest and juice of two limes
¼	cup tequila

Cook pasta according to package directions. Melt butter in skillet and saute shrimp until just pink. Add salt and pepper, jalapeños, green onion, lime zest and juice. Sauté one minute. Add tequila and flame carefully with a long taper match. Serve over fettucini.
Yield: 6 servings

BARBECUED SHRIMP

2	sticks butter	
½	cup olive oil	
4	tablespoons minced garlic	
4	tablespoons cracked black pepper	
¾	cup bourbon	
4	tablespoons Worcestershire sauce	
2	tablespoons dried basil	
1	tablespoon dried thyme	
1	tablespoon Louisiana Gold Pepper Sauce	
	dash salt	
½	teaspoon cayenne pepper	
3	pounds (21-25 count) large shrimp, head on	

Preheat oven to 375°. In a heavy bottom sauté pan, heat butter and olive oil over medium high heat. Combine remaining ingredients, except shrimp, and blend well into butter mixture. Cook one to two minutes. Place head-on shrimp in a large baking pan with a one inch lip. Pour melted butter mixture on top of shrimp, coating as evenly as possible. Place shrimp on center rack of oven and bake three to five minutes or until shrimp are pink and curly. Turn shrimp one time, baste well and allow to cook three to five additional minutes. Remove from oven and serve in soup bowls with the seasoned butter mixture. Hot French bread should accompany this dish.

Yield: 6 servings

TERIYAKI FISH STEAKS

4	fish steaks (any type)	
	salt and pepper to taste	
	flour	
	oil	
½	cup celery, chopped	
½	cup scallions, chopped	
3	tablespoons wine vinegar	
2	tablespoons soy sauce	
½	teaspoon dry mustard	
	sugar	

Rinse fish and pat dry. Season with salt and pepper and dredge lightly in flour. Heat oil and sauté fish until brown on both sides. Add celery and scallions and saute a few minutes longer. Meanwhile, mix vinegar and soy sauce. Dissolve dry mustard and pinch of sugar and pour over fish in skillet. Lower heat and cook five to ten minutes, basting with sauce occasionally. Serve with rice.

Yield: 4 servings

OVEN FRIED FISH

2	pounds fish fillets
1 ½	cups round buttery crackers, crushed
1	tablespoon salt
1	teaspoon black pepper
¼	teaspoon garlic powder
½	cup milk
1	egg
⅓	cup butter, melted
2	tablespoons lemon juice
	Parmesan cheese

Heat oven to 500°. Mix together crackers, salt, pepper and garlic powder. Dip fish in milk and egg, then coat with crumb mixture. Place in well-greased baking pan 9 x 13-inch baking dish. Pour melted butter and lemon juice over fish. Sprinkle with Parmesan cheese and left over crumbs. Place pan on rack slightly above middle of oven. Bake uncovered ten to twelve minutes or until fish flakes easily with a fork.

Yield: 6 servings

FLOUNDER FILLETS WITH SHRIMP SAUCE

4-6	flounder fillets, fresh or frozen
1	teaspoon vinegar
1	teaspoon shrimp boil water
1	(3-ounce) can tiny shrimp
1	(4-ounce) jar mushrooms, sliced
1	tablespoon Worcestershire sauce
½	(10 ½-ounce) can cream of shrimp soup
1	medium tomato, peeled and finely diced
	pinch of garlic salt
	pinch of hot pepper sauce
	pinch of fresh ground pepper
	pinch of red pepper flakes
	pinch of dried cilantro

Before preparing remaining ingredients, wash and drain shrimp and soak 30 minutes in a solution of one teaspoon vinegar, one teaspoon shrimp boil and enough water to cover shrimp. If flounder is frozen, thaw in a pan of water with a little vinegar added. After thawing, cover fillets with milk and soak until ready to cook. This will help remove the "fishy" odor, if the fish is strong. After soaking seafood, combine drained shrimp with mushrooms, Worcestershire, soup, tomatoes and spices to make a sauce. Rinse fillets and place in a two quart dish. Cover with sauce and bake for at 350° for 30 minutes.

Yield: 4 servings

CURRY BAKED FISH

⅓ cup mayonnaise
¾ teaspoon creole mustard
¾ teaspoon lemon juice
¾ teaspoon hot pepper sauce
¾ teaspoon Worcestershire sauce
½ teaspoon garlic powder
⅛ teaspoon curry powder
4 orange roughy fillets
  (about 1 ½ pounds)
2 ½ dozen round buttery
  crackers, crushed

Combine first seven ingredients and brush over tops of fillets. Coat both sides of fillets with cracker crumbs. Place fillets, mayonnaise side up, in a lightly greased 9 x 13-inch baking dish. Bake at 400° or until fish flakes easily when tested with a fork. Serve immediately. Flounder, sole, cod, or snapper can be substituted.

Yield: 4 servings

VERACRUZ ORANGE ROUGHY

2 teaspoons olive oil
1 cup onion, sliced into rings
2 garlic cloves, minced
1 cup yellow bell pepper rings
1 (14 ½-ounce) can Mexican style
  stewed tomatoes with jalapeño
  peppers and spices, undrained
4 (4-ounce) orange roughy
  fish fillets
  dash garlic powder
  dash ground red pepper

Heat oil in a large non-stick skillet over medium heat. Add onion and garlic and sauté seven minutes or until tender. Add bell pepper and tomatoes. Cook over medium-high heat for three minutes. Add fish and sprinkle with garlic powder and pepper. Cover, reduce heat, and simmer five minutes. Turn fish over. Cover and simmer an additional five minutes or until fish flakes easily when tested with a fork. Transfer fish to individual serving plates, reserving cooking sauce in skillet. Keep fish warm. Place skillet with cooking sauce over medium-high heat, and cook three minutes or until thickened. Spoon sauce over fish.

Yield: 4 servings

BAKED FISH ITALIENNE

¼ cup butter
3 pounds red fish or trout fillets
¼ cup lemon juice
¼ cup Worcestershire sauce
 seasoned bread crumbs

Lightly brown butter in baking dish in 450° oven. Dip fish in butter to coat well. Arrange in pan. Mix lemon juice and Worcestershire and pour over fish. Bake for 15 minutes or until just done. Baste once or twice with pan juices. Remove from oven and top with bread crumbs. Baste well again. Return to oven for five more minutes.

Yield: 4 servings

POACHED SALMON WITH MUSTARD-GARLIC SAUCE

4 (6-8-ounce) pieces red salmon fillets or cross-cut red salmon steaks
1 cup water
½ cup white wine
½ teaspoon salt

Mustard-Garlic Sauce:
2 sticks butter (no substitute)
2 teaspoons garlic powder
4 tablespoons spicy brown mustard
1 teaspoon red pepper flakes
2 tablespoons white wine (vermouth)
 parsley sprigs

Translated on page 216

Combine water, wine and salt. Place salmon in glass dish. Pour liquid over salmon. Cover with foil. Cook at 500° for ten minutes or until flaky and no longer transparent. To make sauce, combine all ingredients in small skillet or pan over low heat, whisking until blended. Meanwhile, remove fish from oven. Place one serving on each plate. Cover with warm sauce. Garnish with parsley or sprinkle with chopped parsley.

Yield: 4 servings

SALMON TEEPEES

2   (14-ounce) cans pink salmon, undrained
2   tablespoons dried onion flakes
2   tablespoons salad dressing or mayonnaise
2   teaspoons yellow mustard
2   eggs
    approximately 15 to 20 saltine crackers

In a mixing bowl, blend all ingredients thoroughly, except crackers. Crush crackers coarsely a few at a time, adding until mixture is thick enough to mold into the shape of eight "teepees" about two inches across at the base. Bake, covered, in a lightly greased 10x17-inch glass dish at 350° for about 40 minutes. Uncover and broil until the "teepees" are lightly browned. (The "teepee" shape keeps the salmon moist and kids think they are fun to eat.) Serve with macaroni and cheese and baked tomatoes topped with Parmesan cheese and bread crumbs.

Yield: 8 servings

With the building of irrigation canals in Harlingen, cotton was crowned king of the Valley's booming agricultural industry. Once the largest economic generator for the state, it still holds prominent place in the Valley's economy and social life. Starting in 1953, the auctioning of the nation's first bale of cotton became a major civic event. The auction, first bale party, and annual Algodon Ball...algodon means "cotton" in Spanish..are part of Harlingen's cultural history.

PECAN CRUSTED SALMON
WITH SORREL SAUCE

½   cup pecans
1 ½ teaspoons fresh tarragon,
     chopped (or ½ teaspoon dried)
1 ½ teaspoons fresh basil,
     chopped (or ½ dried)
1   tablespoon butter, softened
4   (6-ounce) salmon fillets

Sauce:
½   cup (packed) fresh sorrel or
     spinach, chopped
2   tablespoons dry white wine
1 ½ teaspoons shallots, minced
1   cup whipping cream
1 ½ teaspoons fresh lime juice
     ground white pepper

Finely grind pecans, tarragon and basil in a food processor. Blend in butter and season with salt and pepper. Tranfer to a small bowl. Preheat oven to 350°. Oil a large baking sheet and arrange salmon on prepared sheet. Sprinkle lightly with salt and pepper and spoon an equal amount of nut mixture over top of each fillet. Bake salmon until cooked through, approximately 20 minutes.

To make sauce, combine sorrel, wine and shallots in a small heavy saucepan. Stir over medium heat until sorrel wilts. Add cream and lime juice. Boil until reduced to sauce consistency, about 12 minutes. Transfer sauce to a food processor or blender and puree until almost smooth. Return to same saucepan and season with ground white pepper and salt. To serve, place salmon steaks on individual plates and spoon sauce around fish.

Yield: 4 servings

CRAB CAKES WITH PECAN CILANTRO SAUCE

1   cup seasoned bread crumbs
2   large eggs, beaten
2   pounds crabmeat
1   medium red bell pepper, seeded
     and chopped
1   medium yellow bell pepper,
     seeded and chopped
4   scallions, chopped
½   cup cilantro, chopped
2   jalapeños, seeded and diced
⅔   cup mayonnaise
     salt and pepper to taste
1   cup safflower oil, more
     if necessary

Sauce:
2   cups fresh cilantro, tightly
     packed
½   cup olive oil
⅔   cup pecans
1   large garlic clove, minced
½   cup Parmesan cheese, shredded
½   cup Romano cheese, shredded
2   tablespoons unsalted butter,
     cut in pieces
     salt and pepper to taste

Gently blend bread crumbs, eggs, crabmeat, diced vegetables, mayonnaise, salt and pepper. Mixture should hold together when pressed. Add more mayonnaise if necessary. Form mixture into 18 - 20 thick cakes. Heat oil over medium high, heat in heavy skillet. Brown crab cakes about three minutes on each side or until golden brown. Drain on paper towel and keep heated in oven (low heat) until ready to serve.

To make sauce, coarsley chop cilantro in a food processor. Add remaining ingredients and process to a smooth paste. Season to taste with salt and pepper. Serve beside crab cakes.

GREEN SHRIMP WITH GARLIC AND RED PEPPERS

2	pounds raw shrimp, peeled and deveined	Saute shallots slowly. Add garlic and herbs. Cook for five minutes. Add shrimp and red pepper. Season and cook shrimp for about three minutes. Be careful not to overcook. Add shrimp to skewers with red pepper cubes.
1	bunch parsely, chopped red pepper, cubed	
2	cloves garlic, minced	
1	package shallots, minced	
1	bunch dill olive oil	

Patrick Bauer - *A popular local chef, and currently the Chief Instructor in the Food Service Technology Department at Texas State Technical College in Harlingen.*

In 1928 the Harlingen citizens voted to build a "first class" auditorium to lure nationally recognized entertainment. John Phillip Sousa was the first "big" star to appear on the auditorium stage. Through the years there have been many renovations to bring it into today's high tech world. The tradition that began with Sousa continues with an arts program that includes Broadway shows, symphony orchestra performances, childrens theater, Community Concerts and school events.

Border Favorites

CHALUPAS OF THE SEA

1   cup leftover or fresh cooked fish, crabmeat or shrimp
4   crisp, corn tortillas, cut in wedges
1   (8-ounce) can refried beans
2   cups lettuce, shredded
1   tomato, chopped
½   cup cheddar cheese, shredded
1   avocado, sliced
     Juice of one lime
1   bunch cilantro, chopped
1   small jar tomato chutney

To crisp tortillas, bake at 350° for three minutes. Spread beans on each tortilla. Layer with seafood, lettuce, tomato and cheese. Mix together lime, cilantro and tomato chutney. Serve chutney mixture and sliced avocados with chalupas.

Yield: 8 servings

CEVICHE

1   pound fresh fish fillets, skinned
1   cup lime juice
1   large onion, finely chopped
2   medium tomatoes, finely chopped
1   medium jalapeño, chopped
30   pitted Spanish green olives, sliced
⅛   teaspoon comino
3   tablespoons capers
¼   cup olive oil
1   tablespoon parsley, chopped
1   tablespoon oregano flakes
     salt and pepper to taste

Dice fish fillets into dime-sized pieces and place in a glass bowl. Cover pieces with lime juice and marinate four to five hours at room temperature. Drain and blot off excess lime juice. Combine pieces with remaining ingredients and mix well in a glass bowl. Cover and refrigerate mixture until cold. Serve as a salad or hors d'oeuvre. For variety, chop one or two avocados and add to mixture. Can also substitute cilantro for parsley.

Yield: 6 servings

RANCHERO DIP

2 (8-ounce) packages cream cheese, softened

1 ½ cups picante sauce

chips for dipping

Beat cream cheese in medium bowl with electric mixer until smooth. Gradually add picante sauce until desired consistency and taste. Refrigerate. Serve cold.

GAZPACHO DIP

1 (4-ounce) can chopped green chilis,drained

1 can black olives, chopped

4 avocados, coarsely chopped

½ teaspoon garlic powder

1 teaspoon black pepper

3 tomatoes, chopped

4-5 green onions, chopped

3 tablespoons olive oil

1 ½ tablespoons cider vinegar

1 tablespoon salt

1 garlic clove, minced

Mix all ingredients together. Chill approximately two hours. Serve with tortilla chips.

MEXICAN CORN DIP

3 cans Mexican corn, drained

¼ cup jalapeños, chopped

4 green onions, chopped

1 (4-ounce) can chopped green chilis

¾ cup mayonnaise

1 (16-ounce) carton sour cream

1 ¼ cups sharp Cheddar cheese, shredded

Mix all ingredients and chill. Serve with tostado chips and fritos.

Can be prepared ahead. This recipe doubles easily and is great for a large crowd!!

SPINACH QUESADILLAS

2	tablespoons olive oil
1	medium onion, chopped
2	packages frozen chopped spinach
	pinch nutmeg
	salt and pepper to taste
⅓	cup cilantro, chopped
2	eggs, beaten
1	(12-ounce) package sharp Cheddar cheese, shredded
1	(12-ounce) package Monterey Jack cheese, shredded
	20 flour tortillas
	melted butter

Sauté onions in olive oil and add chopped spinach. Cook slowly for ten minutes. Add seasonings, cilantro and egg. Stir until well mixed. Mix cheeses together. Make a sandwich by placing cheese and spinach on tortilla and top with a second tortilla. Brush melted butter on tortilla and place in hot skillet until medium crisp. Brush top tortilla with butter and flip over in skillet. Slice like a pizza.

Yield: 8 servings

CLARKE'S QUESO

2-3	tomatoes, chopped
1	medium onion, chopped
½	jar jalapeños, chopped
2	tablespoons horseradish
2	garlic cloves, minced
1	tablespoon vinegar
1	bell pepper, chopped
2	pounds processed cheese, cubed

Heat all ingredients, except cheese, in crock pot. Simmer for 30 minutes, stirring occasionally. Add cheese. Stir occasionally until completely melted. Serve with tortilla chips.

For a spicier variety, substitute a whole jar of jalapenos for ½ jar.

GARDEN FRESH HOT SAUCE

2   large ripe tomatoes (preferably homegrown or gourmet variety)
2   medium white onions, peeled
10-12 tomatillos (without husks)
2   fresh jalapeños, seeded
1   (7-ounce) can chopped green chilis
1   (10-ounce) can diced tomatoes with green chilis
1   (8-ounce) can tomato paste
⅓   cup fresh cilantro (or 2 tablespoons dried)
3   garlic cloves
⅓   cup sugar
3   tablespoons garlic salt
1   tablespoon fresh black pepper

Put all ingredients into food processor and blend until smooth. Place into jars and refrigerate. This sauce will keep for two to three weeks in the refrigerator. Best if flavors are allowed to blend overnight. Serve with tortilla chips and other Mexican dishes.

SALSA VERDE

1 ½   pounds tomatillos, husked and washed
3-4   serrano peppers
1   garlic clove, minced
2   teaspoons salt
½   cup cilantro, chopped
2-3   green onions, finely chopped (white parts only)

Fill medium sauce pan with water, add tomatillos and serrano peppers. Boil until tomatillo turns a darker shade of green (approximately 20-25 minutes). In blender or food processor, place tomatillo, serrano peppers, garlic and salt and blend. Add cilantro and continue to blend until mixed well. Pour sauce into a serving bowl. Add finely chopped green onion and mix well.

SALSA ROJA

4 large tomatoes
4-6 serrano peppers
½ garlic clove, minced
½ cup cilantro, chopped
1 teaspoon salt
  dash of garlic powder

Gas stove method: Place tomatoes and peppers directly over flame until slightly blackened. Do the same with the peppers.

Electric stove method: Place tomatoes and peppers on hot griddle or skillet. Cook until slightly blackened.

Broiler method: Place tomatoes and peppers on top rack; broil until slightly blackened.

Stove top method: Boil tomatoes and peppers in water until skin on tomato begins to peel.

Once tomatoes and peppers are cooked, rinse under cold water, and peel. Place in blender and pulse until coarsely chopped. Transfer to bowl; add salt, dash of garlic powder, and chopped cilantro. Mix well and serve. May be refrigerated up to five days. May be served cold, or you can saute it in small amount of oil and serve warm.

PICO DE GALLO

3 medium tomatoes, diced
½ medium onion, diced
4 serrano peppers, finely chopped
1 (10-ounce) can diced tomatoes
  with green chilis
1 ½ cups cilantro, chopped
  dash of garlic powder
1 teaspoon salt
  Juice of one lime

Combine first four ingredients in large bowl and mix. Add cilantro, garlic powder, and salt; mix. Add lime juice; mix well. Refrigerate at least 30 minutes, but the longer it marinates, the better.

Yield: 4 Cups

MANGO SALSA

2   ripe mangoes, diced
½   purple onion, diced
½   red bell pepper, diced
1   tablespoon cilantro, minced
2   teaspoons rice vinegar,
     unseasoned
1   teaspoon fresh lime juice
     salt and pepper to taste

Mix mango, onion and red pepper in glass bowl. Add other ingredients to mango mixture. Salt and pepper to taste. Let stand at room temperature ½ hour before serving. Serve on top of fish or any seafood, chicken or pork.

ASADO SAUCE FOR POULTRY OR PORK

4-5   chiles ancho, dry
1 ½   cups water
1   slice bread, toasted
1   teaspoon vinegar
3-4   garlic cloves
½   teaspoon ground comino
      pinch of ground cloves
2   bay leaves
1   teaspoon thyme leaves
      salt and pepper to taste
1 ½   pounds poultry or pork

Brush chiles clean (if needed). Boil in 1 ½ cups water until soft. Stem and seed chiles. Combine with cooking water, toast, vinegar, garlic, comino and cloves into a blender. Blend until smooth. Add bay leaves and thyme. Blend again. To serve, brown meat in large non-stick skillet with lid. Pour sauce over browned meat and simmer, partially covered about 30-35 minutes, or until meat is tender. Add salt and pepper to taste.

Yield: 4-6 servings

TORTILLA SOUP

1	large onion, chopped	
4	carrots, sliced	
4	stalks celery, chopped	
2	large potatoes, chopped	
4	tablespoons oil	
4	quarts chicken broth	
2	tablespoons chili powder	
1	(28-ounce) can stewed tomatoes	
1	tablespoon comino	
1	teaspoon white pepper	
1	teaspoon garlic powder	
1	can garbanzo beans, cooked	
1	pound fajita meat, chopped	
2	tablespoons fresh cilantro, chopped	
25	corn tortillas, cut into fourths	

Sauté onion, carrots, celery and potatoes in oil until onions and potatoes are soft. Drain and reserve oil. In a large soup kettle, simmer chicken broth, chili powder, stewed tomatoes, comino, white pepper, garlic powder and garbanzo beans. Add sautéed vegetables to broth. Use drained oil to saute fajita meat for five minutes. Drain and add to broth. Add cilantro and tortillas. Let simmer, covered for 30 minutes.

Yield: 8 servings

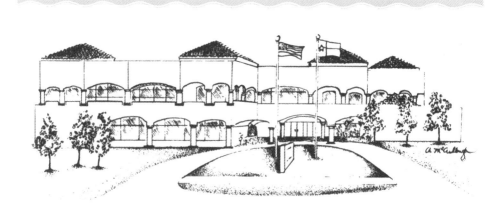

In 1920, feeling the desperate need for reading material, Mrs. F.L. Crown of Harlingen convinced the owner of an empty building to allow her to use it for a "lending library." Collecting books from wherever she could find them, she would open every Saturday from 2 p.m. until 4 p.m. Since then, the city's library has grown and changed locals several times. In 1990, local voters, private donors, banks, businesses...and the Harlingen Junior League...worked together to finance, build and furnish the 46,000 square foot, $4.4 million Harlingen Public Library.

TLANPEÑO SOUP

1	medium tomato
¼	medium onion
1	garlic clove
1	teaspoon chicken boullion
2	whole chicken breasts with bones
1	teaspoon salt
1	small Mexican or medium yellow squash
1	cup corn, drained
1	cup peas and carrots (frozen or fresh)
1	can chile chipotlé
1-2	avocados, sliced
	Monterey Jack cheese, shredded

In blender, puree tomato, ⅛ of medium onion, garlic, chicken boullion, and salt and set aside. Fill two quart soup pot with water and bring to boil. Add chicken. Chop squash into small cubes, and remainder of onion in slices. Sauté all vegetables with small amount of oil in medium skillet until tender. Add tomato puree and two to three chipotle chiles and cook approximately five minutes. Remove chicken. Debone, shred, and return to pot. Add vegetable mixture to chicken soup and cook about 20 minutes. When serving, garnish with avocado slices and cheese.

Yield: 6 servings

With the coming of NAFTA, the Rio Grande Valley is no longer the "backdoor" of our country but has become the "front door" to Central and South America. Scores of business travelers from all over the world are arriving daily to seek International opportunities.

ALBONDIGAS

1	pound lean ground beef
1	egg, slightly beaten
2	tablespoons rice, uncooked
1	tomato, chopped
½	cup onion, chopped
1-2	garlic cloves, minced
¼	teaspoon thyme
¼	teaspoon oregano
¼	teaspoon marjarom
¼	teaspoon salt
2	cups squash, carrots and potatoes, chopped
¼	onion, thinly sliced
1	tomato
1	clove garlic, minced
⅛	medium onion
1	teaspoon salt
1	teaspoon chicken bouillon granules
1	tablespoon oil
2	bay leaves, crumbled
¼	cup fresh cilantro, chopped

Beat egg with fork. Add ground beef, rice, tomato, onion, garlic, thyme, marjoram, oregano and salt. Form into balls about the size of golf balls. In a 3-quart dutch oven or saucepan, add enough water to fill. Bring to boil. Add meatballs, two cups chopped vegetables and ¼ onion. Do not let soup boil fast or meatballs will fall apart. In blender, make tomato puree by adding one tomato, ⅛ medium onion, garlic clove, one teaspoon salt and one teaspoon chicken bouillon. Puree until smooth. In small skillet, heat one tablespoon oil and saute tomato puree for two minutes. Add crumbled bay leaves and cilantro. Simmer two or three minutes. Add tomato puree mixture to soup and cook until vegetables are tender.

Yield: 8 servings

MEXICAN CHICKEN SOUP

2	whole chicken breasts
¼	small onion
1	clove garlic
1	teaspoon salt
1	tablespoon olive oil
1	onion, chopped
2	garlic cloves, finely chopped
1	large red bell pepper, diced
1	quart chicken broth
⅓	cup fresh lime juice
2	chicken breasts, cooked and shredded
1	cup rice, cooked
2	whole tomatoes, chopped
½	cup fresh cilantro, chopped
3	jalapeños, chopped (optional)

Boil chicken in one quart water with ¼ small onion, garlic clove and one teaspoon salt. Remove chicken, onion and garlic from broth and set broth aside. Shred chicken and set aside. In a soup pot, saute onion, garlic and peppers in oil until soft. (Jalapeños can be added at this point.) Add broth and bring to a boil. Add lime juice, chicken and rice; return to boil. Add tomatoes and ¼ cup cilantro. Turn off heat and let stand five minutes. Add salt and pepper to taste. Garnish with remaining cilantro.

Yield: 4-6 servings

TACO SOUP

2	pounds ground beef
1	small onion, chopped
1	(4-ounce) can chopped green chilis
1	teaspoon salt
½	teaspoon pepper
1	package taco seasoning
1	(14 ½-ounce) can hominy, undrained
1	(14 ½-ounce) can kidney beans, undrained
1	(14 ½-ounce) can pinto beans, undrained
3	(14 ½-ounce) cans stewed tomatoes
1 ½	cups water

Brown ground beef, onion and green chiles on medium high heat in a large dutch oven. Stir in remaining ingredients and bring to a boil. Simmer for 30 minutes on low.

Yield: 10 Servings

CHICKEN OLÉ SOUP

2 tablespoons oil
½ cup onion, chopped
2 fresh jalapeño peppers, diced
2 garlic cloves, minced
1 (48-ounce) can spicy tomato juice
1 chicken, cut up
6 cups water
   salt and pepper to taste
2 tablespoons Worcestershire sauce
1 tablespoon steak sauce
½ cup cilantro, chopped

In large dutch oven, saute onion, jalapeño, and garlic in oil. Add tomato juice, chicken and six cups water. Salt and pepper to taste. Add Worcestershire sauce and steak sauce. Cook about one hour. Remove chicken, cut into small pieces and return to pot. Add ½ cup cilantro. Garnish with Monterey Jack cheese, cilantro, avacado, tomato, green onions, sour cream, lime or corn chips.

Yield: 6-8 servings

CHILAQUILES

1 ½ pounds roma tomatoes
1 ½ cups white onion, chopped
2   garlic cloves, peeled
6-8 serrano peppers, to taste
     oil for frying
12   corn tortillas, cut in 1/2 inch strips
     salt to taste
½   cup queso añejo, shredded
     Monterey Jack cheese, shredded

Preheat broiler. Broil whole tomatoes, onion, garlic and serrano peppers on top rack until browned (two to three minutes); turn over and broil two to three minutes more. Let cool; peel tomatoes and serranos and transfer in batches to blender or food processor. Pulse until coarsely pureed. Heat ½ inch oil in skillet over medium high heat. Fry tortilla strips in batches until slightly crisp and golden. Transfer to paper towels to drain. Remove all but three tablespoons of oil from skillet. Add pureé and tortillas and stir gently to combine. Season with salt and heat five to seven minutes. Sprinkle with the cheese and serve.

This is an excellent side dish with Huevos Rancheros!

3	pounds pork espaldilla
1	garlic head
½	medium onion
1-2	teaspoons salt
1	package corn husks (ojas de maize)
4	garlic cloves
¼	teaspoon cumin seeds
4	whole black pepper corns

For salsa Huajillo:

6	chiles Huajillos
1	cup oil
10	small tomatillos
4	large garlic cloves
1	teaspoon salt
3	pounds fresh ground masa
¼	teaspoon baking powder
1	heaping tablespoon salt
1	pound lard
	broth (reserved from boiled pork)
1	cup masa flour

Boil pork in large saucepan with one head of garlic, ½ medium onion and one to two teaspoons salt until tender (45-60 minutes). Soak corn husks in hot water until ready to use.

Prepare the salsa: In a small skillet, add one cup oil over medium high heat. When hot add one chile, quickly turn to other side and remove (be careful not to let them burn). Repeat with remaining chilies. Place in blender. Remove husks from tomatillos and wash. Fill a saucepan ¾ full with water over medium high heat; add tomatillo. Boil until they turn a darker shade of green (approximately 10-15 minutes). Drain. Place tomatillos in blender. Add four cloves of garlic and one teaspoon salt. Blend and set aside. When pork is done, remove from saucepan (defat and reserve broth). Debone and shred (but not too small). Heat large skillet, add two tablespoons oil. Add the shredded pork and sauté. In "molcajete" grind four garlic cloves, ¼ teaspoon cumin seeds, and four whole black pepper corns. Add to pork and continue to sauté another two to three minutes. Add salsa to pork mixture and cook another five minutes. Remove from heat and allow to cool.

Prepare masa: In large bowl, knead three pounds masa for tamales by hand, until it is completely broken up, shift it all to one side of the bowl. On the other side add one pound lard. Work lard with your hands until extremely smooth and creamy. In small bowl, place ¼ cup broth, ¼ teaspoon baking soda, and one teaspoon baking powder. Mix well and add to lard and mix in. Keep remaining broth warm. Add one heaping tablespoon salt, mix slowly. Combine masa and lard, making sure to knead out any lumps. Add ¾ to one cup masa flour, mix. Add ¾ cup warm broth and continue kneading. Add another ¾ cup warm broth and knead (you may add more if needed). The dough should be mushy, but not runny. If it gets too runny add a little more masa flour until you get the right consistency). "Slap" dough around (this will allow it to get fluffy). To test dough for readiness: drop a small piece of dough into a glass of water. If it rises to top, it is ready, if not keep "slapping". Drain water from corn husks. With the back of a spoon, starting with the large end of each husk, spread a thin layer of dough in square shape. Fill each with one tablespoon of pork mixture. Fold left side over filling, then fold right side over to cover the left side of husk. Now fold bottom up.

To cook tamales: In a three quart Dutch oven, arrange tamales standing on the "end". Add enough boiling water to make 1 ½ inches. Cover with lid and cook over medium heat until water

returns to a boil. Reduce heat to medium low and cook about one hour.

Ready test: Remove one tamale and unfold. If leaf does not stick to dough they are ready. Serve with plenty of salsa verde, rojo, huajillo, or pico de gallo.

Variations: Tamales verdes: instead of salsa huajillo, add salsa verde. Tamales de frijol (beans): In a large skillet, add enough oil to cover bottom. When hot, add freshly cooked pinto beans, drained (reserve some liquid). Mash very well. Add one cup liquid. Cook until all liquid is absorbed. You may have to add more oil. Add salsa huajillo.

Tips: This is much easier to do with more than one person, using an assembly line.

To reheat: Place griddle or skillet over medium to medium high heat. Place tamales on hot griddle. Turn until heated (husks will blacken, not burn, giving it a nice crispy texture. Yield: 3-4 dozen

PICADILO CON PAPAS

1	pound ground beef
2	medium potatoes, cubed
	salt and pepper to taste
1	medium tomato
¼	medium onion
1	garlic clove
1	teaspoon chicken bouillon
	pinch comino seeds
1 ½	cups water

Brown ground beef in large skillet, salt and pepper to taste. Add cubed potatoes, stirring occasionally. In blender, puree tomato, onion, garlic and bouillon. Add puree to meat mixture. Mix thoroughly. Add pinch of comino and water. Cover and cook over medium heat until potato is tender. Uncover and continue cooking until desired consistency is reached.

TACO SKILLET DINNER

1	pound ground beef
1	(15-ounce) can whole kernel corn, drained
1	(8-ounce) can tomato sauce
1	cup water
1	package taco seasoning mix
1	(4-ounce) package Monterey Jack cheese, shredded

Brown ground beef in a large skillet; drain off fat. Stir in next four ingredients; simmer uncovered 20-30 minutes. Add cheese and let it melt.

RIO GRANDE CORNBREAD

1   cup yellow cornmeal
¾   tablespoon baking soda
1   teaspoon salt
1   (14 ½-ounce) can creamed corn
1-2 jalapeños, chopped
1   cup buttermilk
¼   cup oil
2   eggs
1   pound ground beef
1   onion, chopped
1   garlic clove, minced
    salt and pepper to taste
¾   pound Cheddar cheese, shredded

Combine cornmeal, baking soda, salt, cream corn, jalapeños, buttermilk, oil and eggs in a large bowl and set aside. In a large skillet, brown ground meat and saute with onion, garlic, salt and pepper. Drain. Grease a large 9 x 13-inch pan. Pour half of the cornbread mixture into the pan. Layer the drained meat mixture followed by the cheese. Pour the remaining cornbread mixture on top and bake at 350° for 55 to 60 minutes. Serve with salsa.

Yield: 8-10 servings

MARVELOUS MEXICAN CASSEROLE

2   pounds ground beef
1   onion, finely chopped
1   (10 ½-ounce) can cream of mushroom soup
1   (10 ½-ounce) can cream of chicken soup
1   (4-ounce) can chopped green chilis
1   (4-ounce) can evaporated milk
1   (8-ounce) can enchilada sauce
1   pound processed cheese, cubed
1   (8-ounce) bag of tortilla chips, crushed

Sauté meat and onion in hot salted skillet until brown. Add remaining ingredients, except cheese and chips. Line a three quart casserole dish with chips and cheese. Pour half of meat mixture over chips and cheese. Repeat layers and sprinkle with paprika or chili powder. Bake at 350° for 20-25 minutes.

Yield: 8-10 servings

MEXICAN CHICKEN ROLLUPS

2   (8-ounce) cans crescent rolls
2 ¼   cups boiled chicken, shredded
1   (4-ounce) package Cheddar cheese, shredded (optional)
1   small jar picante sauce (mild or medium), drained
1   egg white
1   teaspoon water

Heat oven to 375°. Lightly grease cookie sheet. In a large bowl, combine chicken, picante sauce and cheese and mix well. Separate dough into eight rectangles. Be sure to press the perforations to keep from opening. Spoon about ½ cup of mixture into each rectangle and spread to within one inch of edge. Starting at the long side, roll up and pinch edge to seal. Place seam down on prepared cookie sheet. In a small bowl, beat the egg white and water. Brush egg white mixture over each rollup. Bake at 375° for 20-25 minutes or until golden brown. Serve with sour cream, guacamole and black olives.

Yield: 8 servings

According to local historians, the first orange trees were planted in the Valley on the Laguna Seca ranch by Carlotta Vela in 1871. Orange seeds were carried from Spain by missionary priests and presented to the Vela family. Today, despite rare but devastating freezes that threaten the industry, Valley citrus products are known around the world. The Star Ruby and Rio Red grapefruit varieties...prized for their exuberant color and sweetness...were developed by Harlingen's own Richard Hensz, former director of the A & I Citrus Center.

CHICKEN PICANTE

6	boneless, skinless, chicken breast halves
½	cup medium chunky taco sauce
¼	cup Dijon mustard
2	tablespoons fresh lime juice
2	tablespoons butter
6	tablespoons plain yogurt, divided
1	lime, peeled, sliced into six segments, membrane removed cilantro, chopped

In large bowl, make marinade by mixing taco sauce, mustard and lime juice. Add chicken, turning to coat. Marinate at least 30 minutes. In large fry pan, melt butter over medium heat until foamy. Remove chicken from marinade and cook in fry pan, turning about ten minutes or until brown on all sides. Add marinade; cook five minutes more, until fork can be inserted in chicken with ease and marinade is slightly reduced and beginning to glaze. Remove chicken to warm serving platter. Increase heat to high, boil marinade one minute. Pour over chicken. Place one tablespoon yogurt on each breast half and top each with lime segment. Garnish with cilantro.

Yield: 6 servings

Long known as the medical center of the Rio Grande Valley, Harlingen's Valley Baptist Medical Center is the largest general acute care hospital in our area. The 500 bed, state of the art, hospital continues to grow to meet the needs of the community and is a source of great comfort to local patients as well as the large number of Winter Texans.

CALABAZA CON POLLO

1	chicken cut up, or 4 chicken breasts cut in strips
	black pepper to taste
3	cups Mexican squash, cubed
1	can corn, drained or ½ bag frozen corn
1	medium tomato
½	onion, divided in half
1	garlic clove
1	teaspoon chicken bouillon
1	teaspoon salt
2	bay leaves
1 ½	cups water
2	tablespoons oil

Heat oil in large skillet. Sprinkle a dash of pepper over chicken. Cook until golden brown, and drain. Place tomato, ¼ onion, garlic, salt and chicken boullion in blender or food processor and puree until smooth. Set aside. Add cubed squash and thinly sliced ¼ onion to chicken, stirring occasionally until tender. Add tomato puree, saute two minutes. Mix in corn. Add water and bay leaves (be sure to break bay leaves to "release" flavor). Cover and simmer 20-30 minutes until vegetables are tender.

Yield: 4 servings

SOUTH TEXAS ENCHILADA CASSEROLE

3 ½	cups chili meat
1 ½	pounds American cheese, shredded
20	corn tortillas, softened with oil
	oil or shortening
1	onion, chopped (optional)

In a 9 x 13-inch dish, place a layer of softened tortillas and spread alternating layers of chili, cheese and tortillas until casserole dish is filled. Finish with a top layer of cheese. Heat in microwave or oven until bubbling. Serve alone or with rice and beans.

Yield: 6 servings

ENCHILADAS ROJAS

5   chiles anchos
      salt to taste
3   dozen corn tortillas
1   (12-ounce) loaf Mexican style
      cheese (white), or
      Monterey Jack cheese
1   whole chicken, boiled, deboned
      and shredded
1   onion, diced
      Romaine lettuce leaves
      vegetable oil
4-5   garlic cloves

To make sauce, soak chiles in cold water for about 15 minutes. (They should change color. Older chiles may take longer than 15 minutes.) Remove seeds, and puree in blender with garlic. Add salt. Add water if sauce seems too thick. Dip tortillas in sauce and fry in oil. Remove and fill with cheese, chicken and onion. Wrap and place in dish to keep warm. Serve immediately on top of lettuce leaf. For best results, use thin, extra white corn tortillas.

Sugarcane was first introduced to the region in the early 1800's but by the 1920's the last of the sugar mills in the area closed its doors. It would not be until 1973 that a group of 119 farmers formed a cooperative and opened a new sugar mill for the tree-county area. Today, it processes more than a million tons of sugarcane annually from 35,000 acres planted. The burning of the cane during the October to April harvest sometimes creates a light ash that settles on windshields and patio furniture. To the people of the Rio Grande Valley, however, its only a tangible sign of a thriving local industry.

½	pound boneless, skinless chicken breasts
2	tablespoons vegetable oil, plus more for frying
⅓	cup white onion, finely chopped
2	garlic cloves, minced
¼	cup serrano peppers, chopped
½	cup cilantro, chopped
1	recipe Salsa Verde *(found on page 151)*
½	cup thick cream (Mexican crema) Salt to taste
12	corn tortillas
½	cup queso añejo, crumbled or feta cheese, crumbled

Boil chicken breasts over high heat; reduce heat and simmer, covered, for ten minutes until tender. Remove, cool, and shred. Heat two tablespoons oil in skillet over medium heat. Saute onion and garlic until softened; add serrano peppers, cilantro, and shredded chicken and mix well. Remove from heat. In saucepan, heat salsa verde over medium heat five minutes. Stir in cream and salt to taste. Keep warm over low heat. Preheat oven to 350°. Heat ½ inch oil in skillet over medium high heat. Fry each tortilla until softened, but not crisp (five seconds). Transfer to paper towels to drain. Spread one cup green sauce on bottom of a 9 x 13-inch baking dish. Dip a tortilla in the sauce and transfer to plate. Spread with two tablespoons filling and roll up tightly. Transfer enchilada to baking dish seam side down. Repeat with remaining tortillas; arrange in one layer. Pour remaining sauce over enchiladas. Cover with foil and bake 20 minutes. Preheat broiler. Sprinkle cheese over enchiladas, broil on top rack for two to three minutes to brown top.

Yield: 6 servings

ENCHILADAS CHIPOTLE

Salsa Chipotle:

1	can chipotle chiles in adobo sauce (will use 3-6 chiles)
3	garlic cloves, minced
1	teaspoon comino
1	teaspoon oregano
4	tablespoons butter
4	tablespoons flour
1	cup beef broth
2 ½	cups water
6	tablespoons of reserved adobo sauce

Rinse, seed and chop chiles. (Use more chiles for hotter salsa.) In molcajete or with mortar and pestle, grind garlic, comino and oregano. Melt butter in medium saucepan over low heat. Add flour, and cook over low to medium heat until it begins to brown and have a nutty fragrance. Remove from heat, and add broth a little at a time, stirring well after each addition. Return to heat, and add water in a slow stream, stirring constantly. Add chilies, adobo sauce, and garlic mixture, and bring to a boil. Reduce heat, and simmer uncovered, stirring often until sauce thickens, about 30 minutes.

Enchiladas:

	cooking oil
12	corn tortillas
½	pound mild Cheddar cheese, shredded
½	pound cooked chicken, shredded
½	medium onion, minced

Heat about ½ inch cooking oil in small skillet just until it begins to smoke. Using kitchen tongs, immerse each tortilla in oil for a few seconds, until it becomes soft and pliable. Remove, and drain on paper towels. Preheat oven to 375°. Place about a tablespoon each of cheese and chicken and sprinkling of onion on each tortilla, and roll into a cylinder. Place three enchiladas on each of four ovenproof dinner plates. Pour ¼ salsa chipotle over each serving of enchiladas, then sprinkle with remaining cheese and onion. Set plates in oven, and heat until cheese melts and sauce bubbles, about eight to ten minutes. Serve with rice and refried beans or with thin charbroiled tenderloin steak.

Yield: 4 servings

EASY ENCHILADAS VERDES CASSEROLE

12	corn tortillas
1	pint sour cream
1	medium onion, peeled and boiled
12	tomatillos (without husks)
1	(7-ounce) can chopped green chilis
½	fresh jalapeño, seeded
1	tablespoon garlic salt
½	cup Mozzarella cheese, shredded
½	cup Monterrey Jack cheese, shredded
⅓	cup Cheddar cheese, shredded non-stick cooking spray
1	whole chicken

Boil and shred chicken. Stack tortillas and cut into thin small strips 1-2 inches long. Set aside. Place sour cream, onion, tomatillos, green chilis, jalapeños, and garlic salt into food processor and blend until relatively smooth, without large chunks. In separate bowl loosely mix three kinds of cheeses together. Preheat oven at 400°. Spray casserole dish well, including sides. Pour thin layer of sauce on bottom of dish. Create a layer of tortillas followed by chicken and cheese. Repeat process, until all ingredients are used, using sauce to even out layers. Cheese needs to be the top layer. Bake covered for 20 minutes. Uncover and bake for an additional 10-15 minutes, until cheese turns golden brown and casserole is bubbly.

For a lower fat version, use low-fat or no-fat sour cream and low-fat versions of each type of cheese. Do not use non-fat cheese as it does not melt properly. For a spicier version, use an additional 4-ounce can of green chilis and an additional ½ seeded jalapeño. This dish freezes well and can be prepared ahead of time.

Yield: 8-10 servings

BAKED ENCHILADAS

2 pounds ground beef
1 (8-ounce) can enchilada sauce
1 (8-ounce) can taco sauce
2 (10 ½-ounce) cans cream of chicken soup
1 (12-ounce) package Longhorn cheese, shredded
1 package of 10 corn tortillas

Brown meat. Salt and pepper to taste. Add enchiliada sauce, taco sauce and both cans of cream of chicken soup. Cut tortillas into quarters. In a 9 x 13-inch casserole dish, layer ½ tortillas, ½ meat mixture and ½ cheese. Repeat layers. Bake at 350° for 20 minutes or until bubbly.

Yield: 4-6 servings

Wood Stork, White Ibis, Roseate Spoonbills

MAMA'S CHILES RELLENOS

4	poblano chiles
2	eggs (at room temperature)
2	cups queso asadero or ranchero
	flour for coating
1	medium tomato
¼	medium onion, divided in two
1	garlic clove
2	teaspoons chicken bouillion
1	teaspoon salt
2	bay leaves
⅛	cup Mexican squash, sliced

Cook poblano chiles over open flame or on grill/skillet if gas stove is not available. Turn occasionally until all sides are slightly blackened. (This can take a long time if using griddle or skillet...be patient.) Place cooked chiles in a plastic bag and seal for about 15 minutes or until skin loosens. Remove from bag and peel off skin. Rinse. Carefully slice open on one side and remove seeds and veins. Fill with shredded cheese and seal with toothpick. Roll lightly in flour to coat. Set aside. Separate eggs. With electric mixer, beat eggs until peaks form. (If you turn bowl upside down and egg whites do not slide out, they are ready.) Add yolks and mix only until combined. Add teaspoon salt. Dip chiles in batter and cook in hot oil in skillet. Set aside. In blender puree tomato, ½ of onion, garlic, bouillion. In skillet, saute thinly sliced squash and remaining onion and add puree and broken bay leaves. Let cook about two minutes, adding enough water to make saucy. Place chiles in sauce and cook about five minutes. To serve, place chile relleno on plate and top with sauce. This dish is accompanied very well with Mexican or white rice.

Yield: 4 servings

FIESTA CHICKEN CASSEROLE

8	chicken breasts	
1	box frozen spinach, chopped	
1	bag of tortilla chips, crushed	
	Monterey Jack cheese, sliced	
1	(16-ounce) container sour cream	
2	(10 ½-ounce) cans cream of chicken soup	
1	(4-ounce) can chopped green chilis	
½	cup green onion, chopped	

Cook chicken and cut into small pieces. Cook spinach and drain. In a 9 x 13-inch baking dish, layer chips. Top with sliced cheese. Combine chicken, spinach and remaining four ingredients and pour over chips and cheese. Top with tortilla chips and another layer of cheese. Bake uncovered at 350° for 20-30 minutes until hot and bubbly.

This dish freezes well and can be lower fat by substituting low fat sour cream and reduced fat soups.

Yield: 6-8 servings

NANA'S MEXICAN RICE

1	cup rice, long grain	
1	medium tomato	
¼	medium white onion	
1	garlic clove	
1	teaspoon chicken bouillion	
¾	teaspoon salt	
⅛	cup oil (for frying)	
	frozen peas and carrots (optional)	

In blender, pureé tomato, onion, garlic, bouillion and salt. In saucepan, add ⅛ cup oil over medium high heat. When oil is hot, add rice. Stir constantly so that it may brown evenly. (Mom's technique was to stir right, left, center, up, center down, repeat). If you are using fresh carrots, sauté them together with the rice. When rice is slightly brown, drain excess oil and add tomato pureé. Cook until sauce turns darker red (approximately two minutes). Add two cups water and peas and carrots, if desired. Bring to boil. Reduce heat to medium low or medium and cook approximately 25 minutes, until moisture is absorbed and rice is tender.

Yield: 6-8 servings

ARROZ CON POLLO

1   chicken cut into serving size
     pieces or 4 chicken breasts,
     skinned
     salt and pepper to taste
4   cups water
½   teaspoon comino
3   medium tomatoes, chopped
½   cup celery, chopped
2   cubes chicken boullion
½   cup rice, uncooked
1   tablespoon cooking oil
3   medium garlic cloves, minced
½   small onion, chopped

In a dutch oven, sauté chicken until golden brown. Salt and pepper generously. After chicken is browned, add four cups of water. Sprinkle in ½ teaspoon (or more) of comino. Add tomatoes, celery and bouillon cubes. Continue cooking at medium heat. In a frying pan, brown rice in a tablespoon of cooking oil. When half browned, add onion and garlic. Continue cooking until rice is dark-golden brown. Add to bubbling chicken. Turn down heat and simmer for 30 to 40 minutes. Serve with flour or corn tortillas, hot sauce, sour cream and "borracho beans".

Yield: 4-6 servings

CHILE AND RICE CASSEROLE

3   poblano chiles
4   cups white rice, cooked
1   (16-ounce) container sour cream
     (mixed with enough milk to
     thin)
2   cups asadero, ranchero or
     Monterey Jack cheese, cut in
     small cubes

Roast poblano chiles in open flame using a gas stove or on griddle/skillet, until slightly blackened. Place in plastic bag and seal until skin begins to lift. Remove skin, cut open and remove seeds and veins. Cut into long strips. In 9 x 13-inch casserole, layer ingredients in this order: ½ cooked rice, ½ sliced chiles, ½ cheese cubes and ½ sour cream mixture. Repeat layers in same order. Bake at 350° for 25 to 30 minutes.

Yield: 8 servings

SOPA

½   bag Mexican pasta (stars, letters vermicelli, or other small shapes)
2   tablespoons oil
1   medium tomato
⅛   cup onion, chopped
1   garlic clove
1   teaspoon chicken bouillon
1   teaspoon salt
1   cup vegetables, chopped (optional)

Heat oil in medium sauce pan. Place tomato, onion, garlic, chicken bouillon, and salt in the blender or food processor. Pureé until smooth and set aside. Put ½ bag of pasta in the saucepan. Saute until slightly browned. (If you will be using vegetables, saute them first, and then add pasta.) Add tomato puree and allow to cook one to two minutes stirring continuously. Add four cups water and boil over medium high heat. Turn heat down to medium low, cover and cook 20 minutes or until vegetables-tender.

Yield: 6-8 servings

REFRIED BEAN BURGERS

1   (16-ounce) can refried beans or 2 cups fresh refried beans
1   (4-ounce) can chopped green chilis,drained
1   egg, slightly beaten
½   cup dry bread crumbs
¼   cup onion, chopped
¼   cup Cheddar cheese, shredded
½   teaspoon salt
2   tablespoons vegetable oil

Mix refried beans, chilis, egg, bread crumbs, onion, cheese and salt. Heat oil in a 10-inch nonstick skillet over medium heat. Drop bean mixture by four spoonfuls into skillet. Flatten and shape into patties (each one inch thick). Cook about five minutes on each side or until hot and brown. Top with guacamole if desired. Serve on tortillas or hamburger buns!

Yield: 4 servings

FRIJOLES ALA CHARRA

2	cups dried pinto beans
3	garlic cloves
2	teaspoons salt
6	slices bacon, cut in 1-inch pieces
1-2	serrano or jalapeño peppers, chopped
1	medium tomato, diced
1	(10-ounce) can diced tomatoes with green chilis
1	cup beer
½	cup cilantro, chopped

Sort and rinse beans. Cook beans and garlic in water, over medium low heat until tender (three to four hours). Add salt. In a skillet, cook bacon until almost crispy. Add onion and peppers and saute until onion is tender. Add fresh tomato and canned tomatoes, and cook three minutes. Add one cup beer, simmer five minutes. Turn tomato mixture into pot of beans and add cilantro. Cook 20-30 minutes, or place in crock pot. Cook on low until ready to serve.

Yield: 12 servings

The beautiful sandy shores of South Padre Island was for a time considered the best kept secret in the country. A secret no longer, the island is now considered one of the favorite tourist destinations of Texas. A mere forty minutes drive from Harlingen and the Valley International Airport, the deluge of college students from all over the nation and Canada during spring break and Easter week visitors from Mexico attest to the popularity of the Island for fun seeking sun worshippers. Legends of ship wrecked early explorers and buried pirate stashes, sunsets across the Laguna Madre, luxury high rise condominiums, famous fishing tournaments, excellent restaurants, fun night life, and the close proximity to Mexico all combine to make South Padre Island a very special place for families as well as the rich and famous.

BUÑUELOS

2 cups all-purpose flour
½ teaspoon baking powder
2 tablespoons sugar
1 teaspoon ground cinnamon stick
¼ teaspoon salt
1 large egg, beaten
½ cup milk
¼ cup unsalted butter, melted
1 teaspoon shortening
    vegetable oil for frying
1 cup sugar
1 teaspoon ground cinnamon

In large bowl, sift together flour, baking powder, sugar, cinnamon and salt. In small bowl, combine egg, milk, butter and shortening. Add egg mixture to flour mixture. Stir until combined and dough forms. Knead dough on a lightly floured surface for three to four minutes until smooth and elastic, adding more flour if necessary. Cover with plastic and let rest for 20 minutes. Divide dough into 16 equal balls and cover. Heat ½ inch oil in a heavy skillet. On a flat plate, combine sugar and ground cinnamon, set aside. Flatten a ball between palms and carefully pull the dough into a four inch round about ⅛ inch thick. Set aside and repeat. (You can hang flattened dough over the bowl and allow to dry slightly, or lay them flat. They will absorb less oil if you air them first.) Place aired dough in skillet and fry until crisp and golden. Transfer to paper towels and drain. While still warm, sprinkle with sugar/cinnamon mixture on both sides. Repeat with remaining balls. Serve immediately.

Store leftovers in a loosely covered container at room temperature. You may substitute ½ teaspoon ground cinnamon for the 1 teaspoon ground cinnamon stick.

FLAN

¾ cup sugar
4 eggs
1 (14-ounce) can condensed milk
1 (12-ounce) can evaporated milk
1 teaspoon vanilla

Fill a broiler pan with water and place on bottom shelf of oven. Heat oven to 350°. In a saucepan, over medium heat, heat sugar while stirring constantly until it reaches a caramel color. In blender, add eggs, both cans of milk and vanilla. Pour sugar mixture into flan pan, followed immediately by milk mixture. (This is crucial!) Blend. Place pan on upper shelf of oven and bake for 25-30 minutes. Cook until almost firm and brown on top. Let cool for about ten minutes. Use rubber spatula and loosen around sides. Flip it over onto serving platter and chill.

MANGO MARGARITA

1 cup white tequila
½ triple sec
2 ½ cup ripe mangoes, pureed
   (4 or 5, depending on size)
¼ cup fresh lemon juice
½ cup fresh lime juice
¼ cup fresh orange juice
1 pound crushed ice

Place half of ingredients in blender and blend to a slushy consistency. If mangoes are not fully ripe, add more triple sec.

Yield: 4-6 servings

AGUA DE JAMAICA

3   quarts water
1 ½ cups Jamaica leaves
1 ¾ cups sugar

Rinse Jamaica leaves under cool water. Combine leaves, sugar, and enough water to almost fill saucepan. Bring to boil (10 - 15 minutes) until water turns dark red. Strain and add remaining water. More sugar may be added if desired. Serve cold.

Yield: 12 servings

CAFE DE OLLA

4   cups water
⅓   cup dark brown sugar, packed
1   (3-inch) cinnamon stick
8   whole cloves
1   (3-inch piece) orange peel
½   cup dark roasted coffee,
      coarsely ground
     milk or cream if desired

Combine water, sugar, cinnamon stick, cloves and orange peel in sauce pan over medium high heat; bring to a boil, stirring occasionally. Reduce heat to low and let mixture steep covered for five minutes. Remove from heat. Stir in coffee and let steep covered for eight minutes. Strain coffee through seive or cheese cloth into a warm coffee pot.

Yield: 4 servings

ATOLE DE HAVENA

8   tablespoons oatmeal
4   cups water
1   cinnamon stick
4   cups milk
     sugar to taste

Combine oatmeal, cinnamon and water in saucepan. Bring to a boil. Add milk and return to boil. Remove from heat and add sugar to taste. Serve hot.

Yield: 8 servings

Side
Dishes

BAKED ONIONS WITH RASPBERRY VINEGAR

2   medium 1015 onions
1   tablespoon butter
2   tablespoons raspberry vinegar
2   tablespoons sugar
¼   cup water

Translated on page 232

Peel onions, cutting off as little as possible of the root end. Place onions into boiling water and blanch for five to ten minutes, depending on size. Drain, and when cool enough to handle, cut in half and place in baking dish, cut side down. Dissolve sugar in raspberry vinegar and water and pour over onions. Cut up butter and put on top of onions. Bake at 350° for 30 to 45 minutes, basting frequently, until tender.

Yield: 4 servings

BAKED ONIONS AND APPLES

3   large 1015 onions, peeled and thinly sliced in rings
4   large apples, peeled, cored and sliced in rings
2   cups chicken broth
    salt to taste
¼   teaspoon nutmeg
1   cup round buttery crackers, crushed

Layer onions and apples in 2-quart casserole. Pour on broth. Salt to taste. Sprinkle with nutmeg and crumbs. Bake at 350° for one hour.

Great with wild game!

Yield: 10 servings

SPICY CREAMED CORN

¾ cup onion, chopped
½ medium green pepper, chopped
4 green onions, chopped
4 tablespoons butter
1 tablespoon sugar
½ teaspoon salt
½ teaspoon white pepper
¼ teaspoon cayenne pepper
4 cups corn, canned or fresh
1 cup cream, heavy whipping
1 large egg

Sauté both kinds of onion, green pepper and seasonings in butter until onions are softened. Add corn and all but two tablespoons of heavy cream. Simmer gently, covered, 20 to 30 minutes. Uncover for the last five minutes to thicken mixture. Just before serving, beat egg with remaining cream and beat into corn mixture until frothy.

Yield: 4 servings

CORN AND BROCCOLI CASSEROLE

1 (16-ounce) can creamed corn
1 (10-ounce) package frozen chopped broccoli, cooked and drained
1 egg, beaten
½ cup saltine cracker crumbs
2 tablespoons butter, melted
1 tablespoon dry minced onion
¼ teaspoon salt and pepper
¼ cup cracker crumbs
1 tablespoon butter, melted

Combine vegetables, egg, ½ cup cracker crumbs, onion, two tablespoons butter, salt, and pepper. Place in a one quart casserole dish. Mix ¼ cup cracker crumbs and 1 tablespoon melted butter. Pour over vegetables. Bake uncovered at 350° for 35 to 40 minutes.

Yield: 6 servings

BROCCOLI CORNBREAD

1	cup butter or margarine
4	eggs, well beaten
1	cup cottage cheese, small curd
1	bunch green onions, chopped
1	(10-ounce) package chopped frozen broccoli, defrosted
½	teaspoon sugar
2	(8 ½-ounce) packages corn muffin mix
½	cup Cheddar cheese, shredded

Sauté onions in ¼ stick of butter. Mix all of the ingredients together in bowl, using mixer if needed. Add onions and mix well. Pour into 9 x 13 buttered baking dish. Bake at 350° for 35 minutes and until slightly brown on top.

Translated on page 233

CREAMED SPINACH AND CAULIFLOWER

¼	cup butter
½	teaspoon black pepper
1	garlic clove, minced
¼	cup onion, finely chopped
1	cup small cauliflower flowerets
4	cups fresh spinach, chopped
1	teaspoon salt
1	(6-ounce) package cream cheese, softened

In large skillet, melt butter on low heat. Add pepper, garlic, onion, and cauliflower. Cook on medium heat for six minutes. Add spinach and cook an additional 15 minutes. Turn off heat when all moisture is absorbed. Add salt and cream cheese. Stir until cheese is melted. Serve hot.

Yield: 4 servings

MUSHROOMS SUPREME

2	pounds fresh mushrooms, cleaned and sliced
4	tablespoons butter
2	teaspoons lite soy sauce
½	teaspoon garlic powder
1	teaspoon Worcestershire sauce
½	teaspoon cracked pepper

In 10-inch skillet sauté mushrooms in butter about two minutes. Stir in soy sauce. Add garlic powder and Worcestershire sauce and stir until bubbling hot. Sprinkle with cracked pepper and serve as side dish with steak.

Yield: 6 servings

FRIED EGGPLANT WITH TOMATO AND ARTICHOKES

1   large eggplant
    flour
    salt and pepper to taste
    garlic tomato sauce
    artichoke hearts
    fresh basil

Slice eggplant and dredge in seasoned flour. Fry in hot oil until brown and crisp. Serve with garlic tomato sauce, sliced artichoke hearts and fresh basil.

*This recipe is another one of **Patrick Bauer's** specialties!*

EVA CARTER'S CARROTS

1 ½   pounds carrots, peeled and
      sliced ¼-inch thick
1 ¼   cups water
1   tablespoon sugar
1   tablespoon butter
½   teaspoon salt
⅓   cup apricot preserves
3   tablespoons butter
¼   teaspoon nutmeg, freshly grated
¼   teaspoon salt
      dash white pepper
1   teaspoon orange peel, shredded
      lemon juice
      fresh parsley, minced

Cook carrots in water, sugar, butter, and salt until tender. Drain and set aside. Heat apricot preserves. In a skillet, melt three tablespoons butter. Stir in preserves, nutmeg, ¼ teaspoon salt, white pepper, orange peel and lemon juice to taste. Cook until glazed consistency. Place carrots in serving dish and coat with glaze mixture. Garnish with fresh parsley.

Yield: 6 servings

GREEN BEAN BUNDLES

1 pound fresh green beans, cooked
6 slices bacon, uncooked
½ cup packed brown sugar
6 tablespoons butter
garlic powder to taste
salt and pepper to taste

Translated on page 233

Cut bacon in half. Divide beans into twelve bundles and wrap bacon strips around them. Secure with toothpicks. Place in 9 x 13-inch baking dish. In saucepan, melt butter and add brown sugar and seasonings. Heat until sugar dissolves. Pour over bundles. Bake covered at 350° for 35 minutes, basting bundles halfway through baking time. Remove cover and bake ten minutes longer.

Yield: 4-6 servings

ANDREW'S EASY GREEN BEANS

2 cups water
1 pound fresh green beans
2 tablespoons olive oil
½ small onion, finely diced
4 cloves garlic, minced
1 spring onion, minced
⅔ cup whipping cream
¼ cup sherry wine or
cooking sherry
½ cup Parmesan cheese
salt and pepper to taste

In a large pot, bring two cups of water to a rapid boil. Add green beans and cook four minutes. Add garlic and spring onion and cook another two minutes. Add cream and reduce for two minutes. Pour in green beans and sherry and reduce for two minutes or until cream sticks to green beans. Remove from heat and add Parmesan cheese. Salt and pepper to taste.

Great with turkey, chicken and steak.

Yield: 4-6 servings

GREEN-CHILI CHEDDAR POTATOES

1	cup oil (corn or vegetable)
3	Idaho potatoes, peeled and diced into ¼ inch cubes
1	cup whipping cream
1	poblano chile, roasted, deseeded and diced small
½	cup Cheddar cheese, shredded
½	bunch cilantro, chopped
	salt and pepper to taste

Heat 1 cup oil over medium high heat. Fry potatoes until golden brown. In separate frying pan over medium high heat, add cream and poblano chile. Reduce by ¼. Add potatoes and reduce by ¼ again. Add cheese and reduce heat to low, only stirring cheese until blended. Turn heat off. Add salt, pepper and cilantro. *Do not add cheese on high heat or cheese will break and become gritty!!*

TEXAS POTATOES

1	(2-pound) package frozen hash browned potatoes, thawed
1	cup butter, melted
1	teaspoon salt
¼	teaspoon pepper
½	cup onion, chopped
1	can cream of chicken soup
1	(8-ounce) carton sour cream

Spread thawed potatoes in 9 x 13-inch baking dish. Combine remaining ingredients in a bowl and pour over potatoes. Bake uncovered at 350° for 45 minutes.

Yield: 6-8 servings

SOUFFLE DE POMME DE TERRE

6	white potatoes, medium
4	tablespoons butter
1	teaspoon salt
¼	teaspoon white pepper
	pinch of grated nutmeg
¾	cup light cream
2	eggs
2	egg yolks
	sour cream

Pare and dice potatoes and place into boiling salted water. When tender, drain water and shake dry. Beat potatoes together with butter, salt, pepper, nutmeg, cream, eggs and egg yolks. When light and fluffy, place in souffle dish and frost top with sour cream to taste.

SWEET POTATO CASSEROLE

2	(29-ounce) cans sweet potatoes	Mash all ingredients together. Place in
¼	cup butter	baking dish and bake at 325° for 30
1	cup brown sugar	minutes. Top with marshmallows
1	(8-ounce) can crushed pineapple	after removing from oven.
1	package small marshmallows	
1	tablespoon vanilla	
1	tablespoon cinnamon	

HERBED TOMATOES

6	whole tomatoes, medium	Dip tomatoes in boiling water, then
⅔	cup vegetable oil	remove skin. Combine oil, vinegar,
¼	cup tarragon vinegar	thyme, salt and pepper in small bowl,
	dash of dried thyme or marjoram	set aside. Place skinned tomatoes in
1	teaspoon salt	shallow dish and cover with vinegar
¼	teaspoon black pepper, course	mixture. Chill two to three hours,
⅓	cup parsley, finely chopped	turning occasionally. Remove before
⅓	cup green onions, finely chopped	serving and sprinkle tomatoes with
		parsley and onions.

FORGOTTEN TOMATOES

8	ripe but firm tomatoes	Cut a slice from top of tomatoes and
2	tablespoons olive oil	discard. Drizzle with olive oil and
1	teaspoon Italian seasoning	sprinkle with seasoning and cheese.
3	tablespoons Parmesan cheese	Broil on middle rack till bubbly and
		brown. Can also be baked at 350° for
		15 minutes.

For variety, omit Italian seasoning and cheese and substitute ½ teaspoon garlic powder and two tablespoons Dijon mustard.

Yield: 8 servings

ASPARAGUS WITH FRESH TOMATOES AND BASIL

1	pound fresh asparagus
1	tablespoon olive oil
½	onion, finely chopped
4	cloves garlic, minced
3	fresh tomatoes, finely chopped
1	bunch fresh basil, chopped
¼	cup white white
2	tablespoons butter

Translated on page 234

Blanch asparagus by putting in rapidly boiling water. Cook two to three minutes, drain in colander and place asparagus into ice cold water. This will keep the asparagus a bright green color. If the water is not ice cold it will cause the asparagus to turn brown.

In a sauté pan, heat one tablespoon olive oil. When hot, add chopped onions and sauté two minutes. Add garlic and sauté one minute more. Add tomato, basil, and white wine and reduce for three minutes. Turn off heat and stir in butter, to slightly thicken sauce. Do not bring to boil. Serve sauce over asparagus.

Yield: 4-6 servings

HOLIDAY SQUASH

4	cups yellow squash, sliced
4	cups zucchini, sliced
3	slices bacon, uncooked and chopped
½	purple onion, thinly sliced
1	can cream of celery soup
¼	cup pimento, chopped
½	cup Parmesan cheese

Cook and drain squash. Fry bacon and set aside. Sauté onions in drippings. Add bacon, onions and remaining ingredients to squash. Blend well, then pour into 9 x 13-inch dish and sprinkle with Parmesan cheese. Bake at 350° for 30 minutes or until hot and bubbly.

WESTERN SQUASH

10   yellow squash, sliced
1   small onion, chopped
1   (4-ounce) can chopped
    green chilis
2 ½   cups Cheddar cheese, shredded
    salt
    pepper

Boil squash and onion until tender. Drain well and mash up squash. Stir in green chilis and half of cheese. Pour into casserole dish. Season with salt and pepper. Sprinkle remaining cheese on top. Bake at 350° for 30 minutes.

Yield: 4-6 servings

OKRA PATTIES

1   pound fresh okra, chopped
½   cup onion, chopped
1   teaspoon salt
½   teaspoon pepper
½   cup water
1   egg
½   cup flour
1   teaspoon baking powder
½   cup corn meal

Combine okra and onions. Mix with salt, pepper, water and egg. Mix flour, baking powder and corn meal and add to okra mixture. Drop by teaspoonful into hot grease and brown well. Drain on paper towels.

Yield: 8 servings

SPICY FRENCH RICE

4   large okra, diced
1   medium onion, diced
3   cloves garlic, thinly sliced
2   tomatoes, diced
3   tablespoons butter
1   cup rice
1   can oyster stew
1   teaspoon cumin, crushed
2   sprinkles soy sauce
1   egg, beaten

Sauté okra, onions, garlic, and tomatoes in butter until crisp. Add rice and brown over medium heat. Add oyster stew, soy sauce, cumin and beaten egg. Cover and cook on low heat 25 to 30 minutes.

MUSHROOM RICE

1   cup rice
1   can beef consomme
1   package French onion soup
2   (4 ½-ounce) jars mushrooms, sliced
½   cup margarine

Combine all ingredients in a 2-quart saucepan and cover. Over medium heat, bring to boil. Cook additional 15 minutes over low heat.

Yield: 6 servings

GREEN RICE

5   cups rice, cooked
1   cup milk
½   cup salad oil
1   cup parsley, chopped
2   (4-ounce) cans chopped green chilis
1   teaspoon garlic powder
½   teaspoon salt
½   teaspoon fine black pepper
1   pound sharp Cheddar cheese, shredded

Combine all ingredients. Mix well and pour into a 3-quart casserole. Bake at 350° for one hour.

Yield: 12-15 servings

WILD RICE CASSEROLE

1   box long grain and wild rice
1   cup green onions, chopped
½   pound fresh mushrooms, sliced
1   stick butter
½   cup fresh parsley, snipped
1   cup pecans, chopped
1   cup white raisins (optional)

Cook wild rice according to box directions. Saute green onions and mushrooms in butter until soft. Add in parsley and pecans and mix with rice until blended well. Pour into a 2-qt. casserole and bake uncovered at 350° for 30 minutes. Can be stored in refrigerator until ready to bake.

Yield: 6 servings

Junior League of Harlingen

Founded by 58 charter members in 1947, the Junior Service League of Harlingen become affiliated with the Association of Junior Leagues in 1985.

Throughout the years, the League has made significant contributions to the cultural, educational, and charitable growth of Harlingen. Major projects founded by the League have included: an outpatient clinic for crippled children, a group organized to assist the polio ward at the hospital, a summer reading program and story time at the library, restoration of the Lon C. Hill Home, a music and art appreciation program for the schools, a pre-school center for the deaf, and Rio Fest. Members have assisted with the South Texas Artmobile, the Rio Grande Valley Music Festival Pops Concert, the Cotton Style Show, Tourist Center, and many more community events. League volunteers have served on community boards and chaired events for the T.B. Hospital, Valley Baptist Hospital, and Christmas parade.

Fund raising projects have included the Thrift Shop, Party Props, Follies Revenue, Charity Balls, and raffles. In addition to funding the League's major projects, profits have gone for scholarships, to furnish a ward and maternity room at the Valley Baptist Hospital, help fund a new animal shelter, furnish a children's section in the Lon C. Hill Library, and to assist many other worthy causes.

The publication of this cookbook is in celebration of the 50th Anniversary of our League.

Desserts

APPLE CAKE

4	cups Winesap apples, finely chopped
2	cups sugar
2	eggs, separated
1	cup vegetable oil
2 ½	cups flour
2	teaspoons baking soda
1	teaspoon salt
2	teaspoons cinnamon
1	cup pecans, chopped
1	cup powdered sugar
	juice of one lemon

Mix apples and sugar, set aside. Beat egg whites until stiff, add yolks and beat well. Add oil to eggs and mix well. Let stand. Add oil and egg mixture to apples and sugar. Add dry ingredients and nuts, stirring well. Pour into well greased and floured bundt pan. Bake at 350° for one hour or until done. While cake is baking, dissolve powdered sugar in juice of lemon. Turn cake onto cake plate and poke fork tines into cake, making small holes in cake top. While still hot, using a pastry brush, brush lemon juice mixture all over cake. For lower fat cake, substitute applesauce for oil.

Yield: 12-16 servings

BEST FUDGE CAKE

3	(1-ounce) squares unsweetened chocolate	Melt chocolate and set aside to cool. Cream margarine. Gradually add brown sugar and beat well. Add eggs, one at a time. Add chocolate and vanilla and mix well. Combine flour, soda, and salt and add to the creamed mixture alternately with sour cream. Stir in boiling water. Pour into two greased and floured pans and bake at 350° for 30 to 35 minutes. Cool completely and split in half. Spread filling between layers and then frost.
½	cup margarine	
2 ¼	cups brown sugar, firmly packed	
3	eggs	
1 ½	teaspoons vanilla	
2 ¼	cups flour, sifted	
2	teaspoons baking soda	
½	teaspoon salt	
1	(8-ounce) container of sour cream	
1	cup boiling water	

Filling:

½	cup whipping cream	Whip cream and add vanilla. Whip until foam. Gradually add powdered sugar and beat until soft peaks form.
1	teaspoon vanilla	
½	cup powdered sugar	

Frosting:

½	cup margarine, softened	Mix together. Add two teaspoons whipping cream if frosting is too stiff. Frost on cake and top with chocolate shavings.
5	cups powdered sugar	
¼	cup cocoa	
¼	cup strong coffee	
2	teaspoons vanilla	

Translated on page 220

PERFECT CHOCOLATE CAKE

Cake:
1   cup unsifted unsweetened cocoa
2   cups boiling water
2 ¾ cups flour, sifted
2   teaspoons baking soda
½   teaspoon salt
½   teaspoon baking powder
1   cup butter or margarine, softened
2 ½ cups sugar
1 ½ teaspoons vanilla
4   eggs

Frosting:
1   (6-ounce) package semi-sweet
     chocolate pieces
½   cup light cream
1   cup butter or margarine
2 ½ cups powdered sugar, unsifted

Filling:
1   cup heavy cream, chilled
¼   cup sugar
1   teaspoon vanilla

Preheat oven to 350°. Grease and flour three 9-inch round cake pans. In medium bowl, combine cocoa and boiling water, mixing with wire whisk until smooth. Cool completely. Sift flour, soda, salt and baking powder. Set aside. In large bowl , beat at high speed butter, sugar, eggs and vanilla, scraping bowl occasionally, until light and fluffy, about five minutes. At low speed, beat in the flour mixture (in fourths), alternating with the cocoa mixture (in thirds). Divide evenly into

pans, smooth tip with spatula. Bake for 25 to 30 minutes or until surface springs back when gently pressed. Cool in pans for ten minutes. Carefully loosen sides with spatula and remove from pans to finish cooling on racks.

Frosting:
In medium saucepan, combine chocolate pieces, cream and butter, stir over medium heat until smooth. Remove from heat. With whisk, blend in powdered sugar. Turn into bowl and place over ice. Beat until frosting holds shape.

Filling:
Whip cream with sugar and vanilla.

To assemble:
On plate, place a layer of cake, top side down, spread with half of filling. Place second layer, top side down, spread with rest of filling. Place third later, top side up. With metal spatula, frost sides of cake first, covering filling. Use rest of frosting on top, swirling decoratively. Refrigerate at least one hour before serving. To cut, use a thin-edged sharp knife and slice with a sawing motion.

RED VELVET CAKE WITH ICING

1 ½   cups sugar
½   cup shortening
2   eggs
2   cups flour
1   teaspoon salt
1   tablespoon cocoa
1   cup buttermilk
1   teaspoon vanilla
1   ounce red food coloring
1   teaspoon baking soda mixed
   with one tablespoon vinegar

Cream sugar and shortening, add eggs and beat well. Sift together flour, salt and cocoa. Add alternately with buttermilk to creamed mixture. Add vanilla and red food coloring. Mix well. Fold in soda and vinegar. Do not beat the batter. Pour into greased and floured 9 x 13-inch baking pan. Bake at 350° for 30 minutes. Test with toothpick for doneness. Let cool before icing.

Icing:
1   cup milk
¼   teaspoon salt
¼   cup flour
1   cup sugar
1   cup butter
2   teaspoon vanilla
   flaked coconut

Icing:
Boil milk, salt and flour until thickened. Cover and chill. In a bowl, combine sugar, butter and vanilla, beating until fluffy. Add boiled mixture and continue beating until very fluffy. Spread on cake and sprinkle with coconut.

COLLEEN'S CARROT CAKE

2 cups flour
2 cups sugar
2 teaspoons baking soda
1 teaspoon salt
2 teaspoons cinnamon
4 eggs
1 cup oil
4 cups raw carrots, shredded
½ cup pecans, chopped

Cream Cheese Frosting:
1 (8-ounce) package cream cheese, room temperature
6 tablespoons unsalted butter
3 cups powdered sugar
1 teaspoon maple flavoring

Combine dry ingredients. Beat eggs until frothy, and slowly add oil. Add sugar and flour mixture and then carrots and nuts. Pour into three 8-inch cake pans. Bake at 350° for 25 to 30 minutes.

Cream Cheese Frosting:
Mix together all ingredients and blend until smooth and creamy. Spread evenly between layers and on top and sides of cake.

To decorate, sprinkle chopped pecans on top.

Translated on page 219

BUTTERMILK POUND CAKE

2 ½ cups sugar
½ cup shortening
½ cup butter
4 eggs
1 teaspoon vanilla
½ teaspoon lemon flavoring
3 cups flour
½ teaspoon baking soda
1 cup buttermilk

Cream together sugar, shortening and butter until light and fluffy. Add eggs one at a time, beating well after each addition. Stir in vanilla and lemon flavoring and set aside. Thoroughly stir together flour and baking soda. Add to creamed mixture alternating with buttermilk, beating well after each addition. Pour into greased and floured bundt pan. Bake at 325° for a hour to an hour and 15 minutes. Cool in pan for ten minutes. Remove from pan and cool on rack.

RUM CAKE

1	box butter cake mix
1	(3-ounce) package instant vanilla pudding
¾	cup vegetable oil
¾	cup milk
1	tablespoon rum flavoring
1	cup pecans
4	eggs

Icing:

1 ½	cup confectioner's sugar
¾	stick of butter
4	tablespoons water
1	tablespoon rum flavoring

Combine cake mix, vanilla pudding, oil, milk, rum flavoring and eggs. Mix thoroughly. In a greased and floured bundt pan, spread pecans evenly on bottom. Pour batter over pecans and cook at 350° for 45 to 50 minutes.

Icing:
Combine the first three ingredients in a heavy saucepan and cook until it bubbles. Remove from heat and add rum flavoring. Let sit for ten minutes. Remove cake when done and let cool ten minutes. Loosen sides of cake and pour icing all over cake in the pan. Let cool an additional ten minutes and then invert the cake onto a cake plate.

FUDGE PIE

½	cup butter
1	square semi-sweet chocolate
1	cup sugar
2	eggs
½	cup flour, sifted
1	teaspoon vanilla
1	cup pecans, chopped

Melt butter and chocolate in double boiler and let cool. Add sugar. Beat in eggs, flour, vanilla and pecans. Pour mixture into greased 9-inch pie plate. Bake at 325° for 25 to 30 minutes or until toothpick comes out clean. Serve with vanilla ice cream on top or plain.

LEMON CHESS PIE

2	cups sugar
1	tablespoon cornmeal
1	tablespoon flour
4	eggs
¼	cup milk
¼	cup lemon juice
¼	cup butter, melted
3	tablespoons lemon rind, grated
1	(10-inch) unbaked pie pan (can use frozen)

Stir together sugar, cornmeal and flour. Beat eggs until thick and lemon colored. Add milk, lemon juice, melted butter and lemon rind. Blend well. Blend sugar mixture into egg mixture. Pour into pie shell. Bake at 350° for 40 to 50 minutes. Remove from oven and cool completely before serving.

Yield: 8 servings

MILLIONAIRE PIE

1	baked pie shell
½	box powdered sugar
½	cup butter
3	egg yolks
½	teaspoon vanilla
½	can crushed pineapple, well drained
1	cup whipping cream
5	tablespoons powdered sugar
½	cup nuts

Cream the sugar, butter, egg yolks and vanilla until stiff. Pour into pie shell. Mix together the remaining four ingredients. Spread evenly over the pie. Refrigerate for two hours and serve cold.

PUMPKIN PECAN PRALINE PIE

½   cup pecans, chopped
½   cup brown sugar
2   tablespoons margarine, melted
1   (9-inch) unbaked pie shell
2   eggs
1   (16-ounce) can pumpkin
⅔   cup brown sugar
1   tablespoon flour
½   teaspoon cloves, ground
¼   teaspoon mace
1   teaspoon cinnamon
1   teaspoon ginger
½   teaspoon salt
1   cup half and half or milk

Preheat oven to 375°. Mix pecans, brown sugar and margarine. Spread evenly on bottom of pie shell. In large bowl, beat eggs well. Add all remaining ingredients and mix until just blended. Pour into pie shell over pecan mixture. Bake 50 minutes. Cool and serve with whipped cream.

TEXAS GRAPEFRUIT PIE

1   (9-inch) baked pie shell
32   marshmallows, regular size
½   cup grapefruit juice
1   cup heavy cream
2 ½ cups Texas red grapefruit, sectioned and strained
¼   cup coconut, shredded

Cut marshmallows into quarters and melt in ¼ cup grapefruit juice over low heat. Cool to room temperature. Add remaining grapefruit juice, grapefruit meat and cream. Pour into cooled pie shell. Allow to set in refrigerator. Sprinkle coconut over pie just before serving.

NEOPOLITAN ICE CREAM PIE

1 ¾ cups graham cracker crumbs
½ cup butter or margarine, melted
6 tablespoons sugar
¼ cup nuts, finely chopped
1 teaspoon cinnamon

Blend melted graham cracker crumbs, butter, sugar, nuts and cinnamon. Pour into spring form pan and freeze until firm.

Pistachio Ice Cream Layer:
1 quart vanilla ice cream, softened
1 tablespoon vanilla
1 tablespoon almond flavoring
¼ teaspoon green food coloring
½ cup maraschino cherries, drained
and chopped

Mix all ingredients and spread into bottom of frozen crust. Freeze.

Chocolate Fudge Layer:
1 can condensed milk
2 squares unsweetened chocolate
¼ cup water
1 teaspoon vanilla

Melt chocolate in double boiler, add remaining ingredients and cook over hot water until mixture is thick. Let cool and spread over pistachio layer.

Pink Parfait Layer:
1 quart vanilla ice cream, softened
1 teaspoon vanilla
½ cup nuts, chopped
¼ cup chocolate, grated
⅛ teaspoon red food coloring

Mix all ingredients and spread over chocolate layer. Freeze.

Frosting:
8 ounces whipping cream
1 teaspoon vanilla
3 tablespoons sugar

Remove from springform pan and set on serving plate. Whip together remaining ingredients. Spread over cake. Freeze at least four hours. Before serving, remove from freezer to soften a bit.

CHRISTMAS CANDY COOKIES

1	cup butter or margarine, softened
1	cup sugar
1	cup confectioners sugar
1	cup vegetable oil
2	eggs
1	teaspoon almond flavoring
3 ½	cups all-purpose flour
1	cup whole wheat flour
1	teaspoon baking soda
1	teaspoon salt
1	teaspoon cream of tartar
1	cup almonds, chopped
1	(8-ounce) package mini-red and green M&M's or Heath baking bits
	Additional sugar

In a mixing bowl, cream butter, sugars and oil. Add eggs and almond flavoring and mix well. Combine flours, baking soda, salt and cream of tartar. Gradually add to creamed mixture and mix well. Stir in almonds and candy. Chill dough for one hour or until firm enough to handle. Shape into one inch balls and roll in sugar. Place on ungreased baking sheets and flatten with a flat-bottomed glass. Bake at 350° for 15 to 18 minutes or until lightly browned. Cool on wire racks.

These cookies hold up well in care packages. They are always the first to go at any party, large or small!!

OATMEAL PEANUT BUTTER COOKIES

1	cup flour, sifted
½	teaspoon baking soda
¼	teaspoon salt
½	cup shortening
¾	cup brown sugar
1	egg
½	cup crunchy peanut butter
1	cup oatmeal

Sift flour, soda and salt. Beat shortening and sugar. Add egg and beat again. Add peanut butter and mix. Add flour mixture and oatmeal and mix well. Drop by teaspoonfuls onto greased cookie sheet and flatten with fork or bottom of a glass lightly dipped in sugar. Bake at 350° for ten to 12 minutes.

RANGER COOKIES

1	cup shortening	Cream shortening and sugars together.
1	cup brown sugar	Add eggs and vanilla, beating well.
1	cup granulated sugar	Add sifted dry ingredients, oatmeal,
2	eggs	crisp rice cereal, coconut and pecans.
1	teaspoon vanilla	Drop by rounded teaspoonfuls on
2	cups flour	greased cookie sheet. Bake at 325 ° for
½	teaspoon salt	12 to 15 minutes.
1	teaspoon baking soda	
1	cup oatmeal	
1	cup crisp rice cereal	
1	cup coconut	
1	cup pecans, chopped	

SUGAR COOKIES

3	cups flour, sifted	Combine dry ingredients. Add short-
1	teaspoon baking powder	ening, eggs and vanilla to dry mixture.
¼	teaspoon salt	Mix well. Roll or drop on greased
1 ¼	cup sugar	cookie sheet. Decorate if desired.
1	cup shortening	Bake at 350° for 13 minutes.
3	eggs	
1	teaspoon vanilla	

CRUNCHY CHIP COOKIES

2   sticks butter
½   cup sugar
1 ½   cups brown sugar, packed
2   eggs
1 ½   teaspoons vanilla
2   cups flour, sifted
1   teaspoon baking soda
½   teaspoon salt
2   cups quick oats, uncooked
1   (12-ounce) package chocolate chips
2   cups chow mein noodles

Cream together butter, sugar and brown sugar. Add eggs and mix well. Gradually add flour, baking soda and salt. Stir in oats, chocolate chips and chow mein noodles. Drop by teaspoon on a greased cookie sheet. Bake at 350° for 12 minutes.

Yield: 13 dozen small cookies

CARAMEL BARS

1   (14-ounce) package caramels, unwrapped
1   large can evaporated milk
1   box German chocolate cake mix
1   cup pecans
½   cup butter, room temperature
        Cooking Spray

Melt entire package of caramels with ⅓ cup evaporated milk in double boiler or microwave. Set aside. Combine cake mix with pecans, ⅓ cup evaporated milk, and butter in large mixing bowl. Spray 9 x 13-inch baking pan with cooking spray. Pour only enough batter to cover the bottom of baking pan. Bake at 350° for five minutes. Remove from oven and drizzle all of the warm caramel mixture over top of baked cake mixture. Put rest of cake batter on top of caramel mixture. Bake at 350° for 15 minutes. Cool before cutting into squares. Chocolate chips can be sprinkled on top of caramel to make a chocolate caramel bar.

Yield: 24 squares

CHOCOLATE BUTTERSCOTCH BARS

½ cup butter
1 ½ cups graham cracker crumbs
1 (14-ounce) can sweetened condensed milk
1 (12-ounce) package semi-sweet chocolate chips
1 ½ cups butterscotch chips

Preheat oven to 350° (325° for glass dish). In 9 x 13-inch baking pan, melt butter in oven. Sprinkle crumbs evenly over butter. Pour condensed milk evenly over crumbs. Top with chocolate and butterscotch chips and press down firmly. Bake 25 minutes or until lightly brown. (Be careful not to overcook). Cool completely and cut into squares.

Yield: 24 small squares

PUMPKIN BARS

4 eggs
1 ⅔ cup sugar
1 cup cooking oil
1 (16-ounce) can pumpkin
2 cups flour
2 teaspoons baking powder
2 teaspoons cinnamon
1 teaspoon salt
1 teaspoon baking soda

Icing:
1 (3-ounce) package cream cheese, softened
½ cup butter or margarine, softened
1 teaspoon vanilla
2 cups powdered sugar, sifted

In bowl, beat together eggs, sugar, oil and pumpkin until light and fluffy. Set aside. Stir together flour, baking powder, cinnamon, salt and soda. Add to pumpkin mixture and mix thoroughly. Spread batter in ungreased 15 x 10 x 1-inch baking pan. Bake at 350° for 25 to 30 minutes. Cool.

Icing:
Cream together cream cheese and butter. Stir in vanilla. Add powdered sugar, a little at a time, beating well until mixture is smooth. Frost bars and cut evenly into squares.

Yield: 24 squares

GRANNY'S BLONDE BROWNIES

2	cups flour, sifted
1	teaspoon baking powder
¼	teaspoon baking soda
1	teaspoon salt
1	cup nuts
⅔	cup butter or margarine
2	tablespoons hot water
2	tablespoons white corn syrup
2	cups brown sugar, firmly packed
2	eggs, slightly beaten
2	teaspoons vanilla
1	(6-ounce) package semi-sweet chocolate chips

Sift together flour, baking powder, soda and salt. Sift again and add nuts. Melt butter and add sugar, hot water and corn syrup. Stir in eggs and vanilla. Add flour mixture in small amounts, mixing well. Spread in greased 9 x 13-baking pan and sprinkle with chocolate chips. Bake at 350° for 25 to 30 minutes. Cool completely and cut into squares.

CHOCOLATE BROWNIES

4	squares unsweetened chocolate
2	sticks butter or margarine
4	eggs
2	cups sugar
2	teaspoons vanilla
¼	teaspoon salt
1	cup flour
1	cup pecans, chopped (optional)

Melt chocolate and butter until thoroughly melted. In a bowl, beat eggs and slowly add sugar. Add melted chocolate mixture and vanilla. Blend in salt, flour and chopped nuts if desired. Bake at 350° for 30 minutes.

Translated on page 221

BAKED BANANAS

¾	cup powdered orange drink mix
1	teaspoon mace
1	teaspoon cinnamon
6	tablespoons butter, melted
3	tablespoons candied ginger, finely chopped
6	bananas, cut lengthwise

Mix powdered orange mix, mace and cinnamon. Cut bananas in half. Dip banana slices in melted butter, then in orange mixture. Put in 9 x 13-inch baking dish and sprinkle candied ginger on top. Bake at 400° for ten minutes. Serve over ice cream.

BLUEBERRY CRISP

4 cups fresh or frozen blueberries
1 tablespoon fresh lemon juice
¾ cup brown sugar, firmly packed
½ cup flour
½ teaspoon ground cinnamon
¼ cup margarine, room temperature, cut into pieces
¾ cup rolled oats
vanilla ice cream

Place rack in center of oven and pre-heat to 375°. Grease shallow 1 ½ quart baking dish with margarine or spray with cooking spray. Spread blueberries evenly over bottom of baking dish and sprinkle with lemon juice. In a bowl, mix together brown sugar, flour, cinnamon, margarine and rolled oats until well combined. Sprinkle evenly over blueberries. Bake 30 minutes or until top is golden and blueberries are bubbling. Place on cooling rack. Serve warm or hot, with vanilla ice cream.

Yield: 6 servings

Scissor-tailed Flycatcher

COLD AMARETTO SOUFFLE

2	dozen lady fingers
½	cup cold water
1	envelope unflavored gelatin
¾	cup amaretto
6	eggs, separated, room temperature
¾	cup sugar
1	tablespoon lemon juice, fresh
2	cups whipping cream
½	cup almond slivers, toasted
1	small bitter-sweet or sweet chocolate bar
1	tablespoon amaretto

In trifle bowl, stand lady fingers upright around with edges touching. (May need to trim to fit.) In small pan, sprinkle gelatin over cold water. Let stand five minutes to soften. Cook on low heat until gelatin is dissolved. Remove from heat, add amaretto. Let cool in refrigerator until slightly thickened, stirring occasionally. Beat egg yolks in large bowl. When frothy, add ¼ cup sugar and beat until thick. Set aside. Beat egg whites in another large bowl until peaks form, then add ½ cup sugar. Add lemon juice and beat until stiff, but not dry. Set aside. Whip one cup cream until it forms soft peaks. Fold egg white mixture into egg yolk mixture, then fold in cream. Spoon mixture into trifle bowl. Smooth top. Chill until firm, four hours or up to two days.

To serve, whip one cup cream to soft peaks and add one tablespoon amaretto. Ice the top of the souffle or decorate with a pastry bag. Sprinkle with toasted almonds and top with chocolate curls or shavings from chocolate bar. Keep refrigerated until ready to serve.

MANGO DESSERT

1	cup raspberries (fresh or frozen)
¼	cup orange juice
3	ripe mangoes, peeled and pitted
1	(15-ounce) can sweetened condensed milk
	Juice from one lemon
4	tablespoons pistachio nuts, chopped

Marinate raspberries in orange juice. Place mangoes, sweetened condensed milk and lemon juice in a blender and blend until smooth. Pour half of mango mixture evenly into four dessert dishes. Divide ¾ cup raspberries evenly into dishes. Add remainder of mango mixture into dishes. Chill for several hours. Immediately before serving, top with remaining berries and garnish with pistachio nuts.

STRAWBERRY AND LEMON CURD TART

Tart Pastry:

1 ¼	cups flour
1	tablespoon sugar
½	teaspoon salt
½	cup unsalted butter, chilled
2	tablespoons cold water

Lemon Curd and Strawberries:

5	egg yolks
½	cup sugar
¼	cup fresh lemon juice
	zest of 2 lemons, grated
6	tablespoons unsalted butter
4	cups strawberries

Currant Glaze:

1	cup red currant jelly
1	tablespoon fresh lemon juice

Pastry:

Combine flour, sugar and salt in a bowl. Cut butter into bits and drop into bowl. With pastry blender or fingertips, blend ingredients together until mixture resembles small oatmeal flakes. Sprinkle one tablespoon water over flour mixture, stir gently with a fork. Sprinkle another tablespoon of water and stir. Dough should be damp enough to form a rough mass, but not wet; add more water if necessary. Dump dough onto work surface, gather it together and pat it into a cake. Roll out dough on generously floured work surface until ⅛ inch thick and 11 inches in diameter. Put into nine inch tart pan. Pat some of the over hang back in around the edge to make the sides of the tart shell a little thicker than the bottom. Trim any remaining overhang. Line pastry with double thickness of foil in which a few holes have been poked through. Bake at 425° for eight minutes. Remove foil and bake another eight to ten minutes, or until brown and crisp. Cool completely before filling.

Strawberries and Lemon Curd Filling:
Combine egg yolks and sugar in heavy bottomed saucepan. Whisk vigorously for one minute. Add lemon juice and zest and whisk one more minute. Place over low heat and cook, stirring constantly until slightly thickened. Do not over heat or yolks will scramble. Remove from heat and add butter. Stir until smooth. Let cool, stirring occasionally. There should be about one cup. Transfer to a tightly capped jar and chill before pouring assembling tart. Spread chilled lemon curd in cooled tart shell. Slice strawberries lengthwise and arrange on top of lemon curd.

Currant Glaze:
Bring jelly and lemon juice to a boil in small saucepan, stirring frequently. Remove from heat and let cool, but still warm. If glaze thickens., reheat to liquefy. Pour glaze over lemon and strawberries.

PEPPERMINT ICE CREAM

1   pound peppermint candy, crushed
1 ¾   quart milk
1   pint half and half
1   cup whipping cream

Gently heat in sauce pan milk, half and half cream and whipping cream. Melt the crushed candy in the milk mixture. After the milk and cream mixture cools, freeze.

CHOCOLATE - CARAMEL FLAN

½   cup sugar
1   can sweetened condensed milk
1   cup milk
3   eggs
3   egg yolks
1   teaspoon Mexican vanilla

Caramel Sauce:
½   cup plus 2 tablespoons sugar
⅓   cup water
½   cup plus 2 tablespoons whipping cream

Chocolate Sauce:
½   cup plus 2 tablespoons whipping cream
5   ounces bittersweet or semi-sweet chocolate, chopped

Preheat oven to 350°. Sprinkle sugar evenly in 9-inch cake pan and place over medium heat. Using oven mitts, caramelize the sugar by shaking the pan occasionally until the sugar is melted and has turned a light golden brown. Allow to cool. Blend the remaining ingredients at high speed for fifteen seconds. Pour this over the caramelized sugar. Cover the pan with aluminum foil and place in a larger shallow pan with about one inch of hot water. Bake 45 to 55 minutes or until a knife inserted near the center comes out clean. Remove pan from water and uncover to cool. Loosen edges with a knife. Place serving plate upside down on top of cake pan and quickly invert the flan onto the plate.

Caramel Sauce:
Stir sugar and water in heavy medium saucepan over low heat until sugar dissolves. Increase heat and boil without stirring until syrup turns deep amber, occasionally swirling pan and brushing down sides of pan with wet pastry brush, about six minutes. Remove from heat. Carefully add cream (mixture will bubble vigorously) Place pan over low heat and stir until caramel bits melt and mixture is smooth. Remove from heat and let cool to room temperature.

Chocolate Sauce:
Bring cream to a simmer in a heavy small saucepan. Remove from heat. Add chocolate, stir well until chocolate melts and mixture is smooth. Cool.

To serve, spoon caramel over the top of the inverted flan. Refrigerate until set, about thirty minutes. Spoon the chocolate over caramel. Refrigerate until set, about 30 minutes. Keep refrigerated until ready to serve. This can be prepared several hours ahead of time.

Yield: 6-8 servings

VANN'S CHEESECAKE

Crust:
1   cup flour
½   cup butter, softened
¼   cup sugar
1   teaspoon lemon or lime rind
1   egg yolk
¼   teaspoon vanilla
     dash of salt

Filling:
4   eggs, well beaten
2   (8-ounce) packages cream cheese
1   cup sugar
¼   teaspoon salt
2   teaspoons vanilla
3   (8-ounce) containers sour cream

Crust:
Butter a spring form pan. Mix ingredients with a fork. Press mixture to the bottom and sides of pan. Bake at 400° for nine minutes. Cool before filling.

Filling:
Mix eggs, cream cheese and sugar. Add salt and beat well. Blend in sour cream and vanilla. Pour into crust in the spring form pan. Bake at 350° for one hour. Turn oven off and cool in oven another hour. Refrigerate before serving. May garnish with fresh strawberries.

Yield: 12 servings

PUMPKIN CHEESECAKE

1   cup gingersnap crumbs
½   cup pecans, finely chopped
3   tablespoons margarine
2   (8-ounce) packages cream cheese, softened
½   cup sugar
1   teaspoon vanilla
2   eggs
1   (16-ounce) can pumpkin
1   (5-ounce) can evaporated milk
½   cup sugar
2   eggs, slightly beaten
1   teaspoon cinnamon
¼   teaspoon ginger
¼   teaspoon nutmeg
     dash of salt

Combine crumbs, pecans and margarine. Press into bottom of nine inch spring form pan. Combine cream cheese, sugar and vanilla, mixing until well blended. Add egg and mix well. Pour over crust. Combine remaining ingredients, mix well. Carefully pour over cream cheese mixture. Bake at 325° for one hour and 30 to 35 minutes or until set. Loosen cake from rim of pan and cool before removing the rest of way. Chill.

NUT CRUNCH

1 ¼ cup sugar
¾ cup butter
1 ½ teaspoons salt
¼ cup water
½ cup unblanched almonds
(whole or slivered)
½ teaspoon baking soda
½ cup blanched almonds
½ cup pecans
⅓ cup chocolate chips
½ cup finely chopped nuts

Translated on page 221

In a heavy sauce pan, mix first five ingredients. Boil on medium to medium high heat, stirring often to 290° (using a candy thermometer). Remove and stir in soda, almonds and pecans. Pour into a well-greased 15 x 10-inch pan. Sprinkle chocolate chips on hot mixture. Wait for five minutes. When melted, spread over mixture and sprinkle with chopped nuts. When cold, break into pieces and store in can. (More nuts can be used if desired).

GRILL ROOM BREAD PUDDING WITH BOURBON SAUCE

1 Baguette, broken in pieces
3 cups scalded milk
½ cup heavy cream
4 egg yolks, beaten
½ cup brown sugar
4 egg whites, beaten stiff
1 teaspoon vanilla
½ teaspoon cinnamon dash nutmeg
¼ cup butter, melted
¼ cup pecans (optional)
¼ cup raisins (optional)

Bourbon Sauce:
1 stick butter
1 cup confectioners sugar
1 egg
2 ounces bourbon

Combine bread, milk and cream and set aside. Combine egg yolks and sugar and mix well. Stir in bread mixture and add vanilla, cinnamon and nutmeg. Stir in butter, raisins and pecans. Gently fold in beaten egg whites. Pour into a 2-quart buttered baking dish and set in pan of warm water about - inch deep. Bake at 350° about one hour or until knife comes out clean.

Stir butter and sugar in a double boiler over simmering water until sugar is dissolved and mixture is very hot. Remove from heat. Beat egg and whisk into mixture. Remove pan from base and continue beating until sauce has cooled to room temperature. Add bourbon and blend well. Keep in refrigerator until ready to serve. Heat gently or let come to room temperature before serving. Enjoy!!!

Doris and Rusty Bentley -*The Grill Room Restaurant is located on South Padre Island, a favorite restaurant of locals and visitors.*

KAHLUA PECAN PIE

1 ¼	teaspoon dry coffee	Mix dry coffee and hot water in small
	few drops very hot tap water	bowl, stir to dissolve. Set aside. Beat
3	eggs	eggs, sugar, corn syrup, melted butter,
1	cup white sugar	cinnamon and Kahlua together. Add
¾	cup dark corn syrup	pecans, salt and concentrated coffee.
¼	cup Kahlua liqueur	Pour into pie shell. Bake at 425° for 10
2	tablespoons melted butter	minutes, then reduce heat to 350° for
	or margarine	25 to 30 minutes. Remove pie from
½	teaspoon ground cinnamon	oven. Serve slightly warm or cold,
1	cup whole pecans	with or without Kahlua whipped
	dash salt	cream.
1	unbaked pie shell	

KAHLUA WHIPPED CREAM

1	cup whipping cream	Whip cream until it begins to fluff.
¼	cup powdered sugar	Add powdered sugar; beat until stiff.
½	cup Kahlua liqueur	Add Kahlua, stir to mix in.

Monica Burdette from The Inn at El Canelo shared this delicious recipe with us. This is one of their customers' favorites--reminiscent of richly flavored Mexican candy!

Best of the Best
of the
en español

ESPAGUETI A LA PROVENCAL

1	echalote[1] grande, picado finamente
1	tomate grande, pelado, sin semillas y cortado en cuadritos
2	cucharadas de perejil, picado
1	cucharada de vinagre de vino blanco
1-4	de taza de aceite de oliva
6-8	almejas gigantes o vieiras (scallops)
6-8	camarones
2	cucharadas de aceite de oliva
1	paquete de espagueti de 12 onzas, cocido

[1] *Escalote - "Shallot" Cebollita alargada y delgada, de apariencia seco por fuera y color morado por dentro.*

Combine los echalotes, el tomate, perejil, vinagre de vino y el aceite de oliva en una sartén mediana. Deje hervir, reduzca el calor y deje hervir a fuego lento cerca de dos minutos. En una sartén grande añada dos cucharadas de aceite de oliva fría rápidamente los camarones y las vieiras a fuego mediano. Cocine el camarón hasta que tome un color rosado y las vieiras se vean opacas. Añada los mariscos a la salsa de tomate y mezcle bien. Vacíe encima del espagueti ya cocido y sírvase inmediatamente.

Rinde: 4 porciones

PAELLA DE MARISCOS RAPIDA

1   cucharada de aceite de oliva
1   pimiento rojo, sin semillas,
     cortado en tiras finas
1   cebolla mediana, rebanada
½   cucharadita de albahaca seca
½   cucharadita de tomillo seco
½   cucharadita de orégano seco
1   hoja de laurel, en trocitos
1   lata de tomates en trozo de 16
     onzas, colados (guarde 1 taza
     del líquido)
3   dientes de ajo, picaditos
1   paquete de corazones de
     alcachofa congelados de 9 onzas
1   ½ taza de camarón, sin
     cáscara, desvenado
1   1/2 taza de almejas
1   taza de arroz de cocimiento
     rápido, sin cocer

Caliente el aceite en una sartén hasta que esté bien caliente. Añada el pimiento rojo, la cebolla, las hierbas de olor, el tomate y el ajo. Tape y deje cocer por cinco minutos, moviendo ocasionalmente. Añada el jugo de tomate y los mariscos. Deje que hierva y vacíe el arroz revolviendo lentamente. Deje que hierva de nuevo. Retire del fuego y deje reposar, cubierto, de 8 a 10 minutos. Sirva inmediatamente.

Rinde: 4 porciones

SALMON ESCALFADO² EN SALSA DE MOSTAZA Y AJO

4	rodajas de salmón rojo, de 6 a 8 onzas cada una
1	taza de agua
½	taza de vino blanco
½	cucharadita de sal
2	barras de mantequilla (no substituya)
2	cucharaditas de polvo de ajo
4	cucharadas de mostaza obscura fuerte
1	cucharadita de hojuelas de chile rojo
2	cucharadas de vino blanco o vermouth
	ramitas de perejil frescas para adornar

² *Escalfar - cocer a fuego lento*

Coloque el salmón en un molde de vidrio para hornear. Combine el agua, el vino, y la sal y bañe el salmón. Cubra con papel aluminio y hornee a 500 grados de 8 a 10 minutos o hasta que se desprenda al toque y no se vea transparente. Mientras que el pescado se hornea, prepare la salsa combinando los cinco ingredientes restantes en una sartén pequeña. Mueva vigorosamente hasta que se mezclen bien. Cocine a fuego lento hasta que la salsa esté caliente. Saque las rebanadas de salmón del horno y coloque una en cada plato. Cubra con la salsa caliente y adorne con ramitas de perejil fresco.

Rinde: 4 porciones

CAMARONES ESTILO NUEVA ORLEANS

1	barra de mantequilla (no substituya)
1 ½	cucharaditas de ajo, picado finamente
1	cucharadita de salsa Worchestershire
1	cucharadita de pimienta negra
1	cucharadita de pimienta de Cayena
½	cucharadita de sal
½	cucharadita de chile rojo molido
½	cucharadita de hojas de tomillo secas, molidas
½	cucharadita de hojas de romero secas, molidas
⅛	cucharadita de orégano
1	libra de camarón mediano, limpio y desvenado
5	cucharadas de mantequilla
¼	taza de consomé de camarón
¼	taza de cerveza, a temperatura ambiente

En una sartén de 12", combine la mantequilla, el ajo, la salsa Worchestershire y las especias. Cuando se haya derretido la mantequilla, añada el camarón y cocine destapado a fuego mediano por dos minutos, moviendo la sartén, sin revolver con la cuchara. Añada cinco o más cucharadas de mantequilla y el consomé de camarón a la sartén, moviendo el mismo sin revolver con la cuchara. Añada la cerveza y cocine por un minuto más. Sirva inmediatamente sobre arroz cocido.

Rinde: 4 porciones

LASAÑA DE MARISCOS ELEGANTE

8   hojas de lasaña, cocidas "al dente"[3]
1   taza de cebollitas de Cambray, (cebollino)
2   cucharaditas de mantequilla
8   onzas queso crema, ablandado
1 ½ taza de queso "cottage"
1   huevo
2   cucharaditas de albahaca
½   cucharadita de sal
     pizca de pimienta
2   latas de crema de champiñones
⅓   taza de leche
⅓   taza de vino blanco
2   latas pequeñas de carne de cangrejo
1   taza de queso rallado "mozzarella"
⅓   taza de queso rallado "parmesano"
½   taza de queso rallado "cheddar" fuerte

[3] *Al dente - tierna pero no blanda*

Dore rápidamente en mantequilla las cebollitas picadas. En una licuadora o procesador de alimentos, mezcle las cebollas en mantequilla, el queso crema, el queso, el huevo, la albahaca, la sal y la pimienta. En un tazón por separado mezcle la sopa, la leche, el vino, los camarones y la carne de cangrejo. Coloque en capas como sigue: Coloque cuatro hojas de lasaña cocidas en el fondo de un molde engrasado. Con una cuchara extienda encima la mitad de la mezcla de queso crema y luego extienda la mitad de la mezcla de mariscos. Repita las capas. Añada el queso mozzarella al final y luego espolvoree el queso parmesano. Coloque en el horno por 45 minutos a una temperatura de 350 grados. Después de sacar del horno, extienda una capa de queso cheddar y deje reposar por 10 minutos.

PASTEL DE ZANAHORIA DE COLLEEN

2	tazas de harina
2	tazas de azúcar
2	cucharaditas de sal
2	cucharaditas de canela
4	huevos
1	taza de aceite
4	tazas de zanahoria cruda, rallada
½	taza de nueces, picadas

[4] *Betún - Recubrimiento, "frosting"*

Combine los primeros cuatro ingredientes. Bata los huevos hasta que formen espuma. Lentamente añada el aceite y el azúcar a los huevos. Añada la mezcla de la harina hasta incorporar bien. Incorpore con una espátula lentamente la zanahoria y las nueces. Vacíe a tres moldes para pastel de 8" y hornee a 350 grados de 25 a 30 minutos. Deje enfriar y cubra con betún de queso crema.

Betún[4] de Queso Crema
1 paquete de 8 onzas de queso crema a temperatura ambiente
6 cucharadas de mantequilla dulce
1 caja de azúcar glass
1 cucharadita de extracto de maple

Mezcle todos los ingredientes hasta que quede un betún terso y cremoso.

EL MEJOR PASTEL DE CHOCOLATE
(Tipo Fudge)

3	cuadros de 1 onza de chocolate amargo	Derrita el chocolate y deje a un lado a enfriar. Bata la margarina hasta que esté cremosa. Añada gradualmente el azúcar moreno y bata bien. Añada los huevos, uno a la vez. Añada el chocolate y la vainilla y mezcle bien. Combine la harina, el bicarbonato de soda y la sal y añada a la mezcla cremosa alternando con la crema agria. Añada el agua hirviendo revolviendo constantemente. Vierta dentro de dos moldes engrasados y enharinados y hornee a 350 grados por 30 minutos. Deje enfriar completamente y corte a la mitad. Unte el relleno entre las dos capas y cubra con el betún.

3   cuadros de 1 onza de chocolate amargo
½   taza de margarina
2 ¼   tazas de azúcar morena o mascabado, firmemente prensadas
3   huevos
1 ½   cucharaditas de vainilla
2 ¼   tazas de harina cernidas
2   cucharaditas de bicarbonato de soda[5]
½   cucharadita de sal
1   recipiente de 8 onzas de crema agria
1   taza de agua hirviendo

Derrita el chocolate y deje a un lado a enfriar. Bata la margarina hasta que esté cremosa. Añada gradualmente el azúcar moreno y bata bien. Añada los huevos, uno a la vez. Añada el chocolate y la vainilla y mezcle bien. Combine la harina, el bicarbonato de soda y la sal y añada a la mezcla cremosa alternando con la crema agria. Añada el agua hirviendo revolviendo constantemente. Vierta dentro de dos moldes engrasados y enharinados y hornee a 350 grados por 30 minutos. Deje enfriar completamente y corte a la mitad. Unte el relleno entre las dos capas y cubra con el betún.

Relleno:
½   taza de crema para batir
1   cucharadita de vainilla
½   taza de azúcar glass

Bata la crema y añada la vainilla. Bata hasta que forme picos. Añada gradualmente el azúcar glass y bata hasta que forme picos suaves.

Betún:
½   taza de margarina suavizada
5   tazas de azúcar glass
¼   taza de cocoa
¼   taza de café fuerte
2   cucharaditas de vainilla

Mezcle junto. Añada dos cucharaditas de crema para batir si el betún resulta muy espeso. Cubra el pastel y añada encima ralladura de chocolate.

[5] *"baking soda"*

BROWNIES DE CHOCOLATE

4	cuadros de chocolate amargo
2	barras de mantequilla o margarina
4	huevos
2	tazas de azúcar
2	cucharaditas de vainilla
¼	cucharadita de sal
1	taza de harina
1	taza de nueces, picadas (opcional)

Derrita el chocolate y la mantequilla hasta que queden bien fundidos. En un tazón, bata los huevos y añada lentamente el azúcar. Añada la mezcla del chocolate fundido y la vainilla. Incorpore la sal, la harina y las nueces picadas si se desea. Hornee a 350 grados por 30 minutos.

"CRUNCH" DE NUEZ

1 ¼	taza de azúcar
¾	taza de mantequilla
1 ½	cucharadita de sal
¼	taza de agua
½	taza de almendras (enteras o en rebanadas)
½	cucharadita de bicarbonato de sodio
½	taza de almendras escaldadas
½	taza de nueces
⅓	taza de trozos (chips) de chocolate
½	taza de nueces picadas finamente

En una sartén de base gruesa, mezcle los primeros cinco ingredientes. Haga que hierva a fuego medio o medio-fuerte, moviendo frecuentemente a una temperatura de 290 grados (usando un termómetro para azúcar). Quite del fuego y añada el bicarbonato de sodio, las almendras y las nueces mientras sigue moviendo. Vacíe dentro de un molde de 15"x10" bien engrasado. Añada los trocitos de chocolate en la mezcla caliente. Espere por cinco minutos. Cuando se haya fundido, extienda sobre la mezcla y rocíe con las nueces picadas. Cuando se enfríe, rompa en pedazos y guarde en una lata. (Pueden usarse más nueces si se desea).

CEBOLLAS RELLENAS

4	cebollas dulces 1015 grandes
	sal al gusto
1	libra carne de venado molida, cocida y escurrida
1	sobre de condimento para salsa "gravy" con hongos
¼	taza de leche
1	huevo, ligeramente batido
½	taza de migajas de pan suaves
¼	cucharadita de salvia
¼	cucharadita de pimienta negra
¼	taza de perejil picado, fresco

Pele las cebollas y córtelas a la mitad. Saque los centros y coloque las cáscaras a un lado. Pique el relleno y mezcle con el resto de los ingredientes (excepto el perejil). Con una cuchara vuelva a rellenar las cáscaras de cebolla y envuelva en papel de aluminio. Selle ligeramente. Coloque en la parrilla de 35 a 40 minutos en carbón a temperatura mediana. Adorne con perejil antes de servir.

Rinde: 4 porciones grandes -8 porciones pequeñas.

CHILI DE VENADO BIG TREE

3	libras carne de venado en cubos
3	libras salchicha de puerco, cruda
2	cucharaditas de aceite de olivo
2	cucharaditas de sal
2	cucharaditas de comino
1	cucharadita de pimienta
⅛	cucharadita de pimienta de Cayena
4-6	cucharadas de chile en polvo
1	lata chica de salsa de tomate
2	tazas de agua
1	cucharadita de ajo en polvo
2	cucharadas de harina de maíz en polvo (cornmeal)
1	cucharada de harina de trigo
1	taza de agua

En una olla grande, dore la carne en aceite y escurra. Añada los siguientes ocho ingredientes a la carne y deje hervir. Haga una pasta con la harina de maíz, la harina de trigo y el agua y añada al chili. Cueza a fuego lento por tres horas.

AVES DE CAZA O VENADO A LA PARRILLA

pechugas de paloma, o ave de
  caza limpias, o
venado, cortado en pedazos
cebolla fresca, cortada en trozos
  de 1 pulgada
rebanadas de jalapeño en
  escabeche
tocino en rebanadas delgadas
paquete de queso crema de
  8 onzas

En cada filete de pechuga de paloma o ave o en cada pieza de venado, coloque un pedazo de cebolla y una rebanada de jalapeño (al gusto). Coloque una rebanada de queso crema encima. Envuelva cada pieza de carne con una rebanada de tocino, usando palillos de dientes para asegurarla. Dore a la parrilla sobre carbón (a fuego bajo) por 10-20 minutos o hasta que el tocino esté dorado. Añada un pedazo de 1" x 1" de queso Monterrey Jack para variar.

PECHUGAS DE CODORNIZ AL ESTILO SUREÑO

8	pechugas de codorniz
½	cucharadita de sal
¼	cucharadita de pimienta
½	taza de harina
½	taza de mantequilla, fundida
½	taza de champiñones picados
½	taza de cebolla picada
1	cucharada de perejil
½	taza de vino blanco
½	de crema para batir
	arroz de grano largo "wild rice"

Espolvoree las pechugas de codorniz con sal y pimienta y revuelva en la harina. En una sartén grande dórelas en mantequilla por ambos lados. Sáquelas de la sartén. Dore rápidamente los champiñones, las cebollas y el perejil en la misma mantequilla. Añada la codorniz y el vino. Cubra y baje el fuego entre bajo/mediano. Cocine por 30 minutos, bañando frecuentemente con la salsa. Añada la crema para batir y cocine hasta que esté de nuevo totalmente caliente. NO DEJE HERVIR. Sirva sobre el arroz.

Rinde: 4 porciones

BROCHETAS DE CARNE A LA INDONESA

1 ½   sirloin de res sin hueso y sin
      grasa
1   diente de ajo, picadito o
      prensado
2   cucharadas de salsa de soya
1   cucharada de aceite para
      ensalada
1   cucharadita de comino molido
1   cucharadita de semilla de
      cilantro molida
10-12 brochetas de bambú largas

Corte la carne en cubos de 1 pulgada. En un tazón, combine el ajo, la salsa de soya, el aceite, el comino y el cilantro. Añada la carne y revuelva hasta cubrir por todos lados. Cubra y refrigere por lo menos dos horas o hasta el día siguiente, revolviento ocacionalmente. Remoje las brochetas de bambú en agua caliente y cubralas por lo menos 30 minutos o hasta el día siguiente. Después de marinar, saque la carne de la salsa y drene brevemente (desheche la salsa). Coloque cuatro o cinco piezas de carne en cada brocheta. Arregle las brochetas en una parrilla ligeramente engrasada de 2 a 4 pulgadas por encima de una cama solida de carbón caliente. Cocine, volteando a menudo, hasta que queden bien doradas y cocinadas al gusto. Sirva con salsa de cacahuate.

Salsa de cacahuate:
1   taza de agua
⅔   taza de mantequilla de
      cacahuate (maní)
2   dientes de ajo, picado o prensado
2   cucharadas prensadas de azúcar
      morena (moscabado)
1 ½   cucharadas de jugo de limón
1   cucharada de salsa de soya
¼ a ½ cucharadita de hojuelas de
      chile rojo.

En una cacerola de 2 cuartos[6], combine el agua, la mantequilla de cacahuate y el ajo. Cocine sobre fuego mediano, revolviendo constantemente hasta que la mezcla hierva y se espese. Quite del fuego y agrege revolviendo el azúcar morena, el jugo de limón, la salsa de soya y el chile rojo. Mezcle bien y sirva con las Brochetas de Carne a la Indonesa.

[6] *1 cuarto (líquido) = cerca de un litro*

LOMO DE CERDO RELLENO

1-2	libra lomo de puerco
½	libra salchichón o embutido
	sal y pimienta
2	cucharadas de mantequilla sin sal
2	cucharadas de aceite
1	taza de champiñones rebanados
½	taza de echalotes rebanados
2	cucharadas de harina
1 ½	taza de leche tibia
2	cucharadas de mostaza en grano

Caliente el horno a 350 grados. Corte un hoyo en el centro del lomo (use el mango de una cuchara de madera) y rellene el lomo con la salchicha. Espolvoree con sal y pimienta al gusto. Ponga a fundir la mantequilla en una sartén. Añada el lomo y dore. Coloque en una charola para hornear. Hornee el lomo hasta que alcance una temperatura interior de 170 (aproximadamente 30-40 minutos). Haga la salsa como sigue: En una sartén caliente el aceite y dore los champiñones y echalotes por cinco minutos. Revuelva la harina. Añada la leche tibia bata hasta obtener una salsa espesa. Mezcle la mostaza. Saque el lomo cocido del horno. Rebane en rebanadas de media pulgada y arregle en un platón de servir. Rocíe la salsa sobre la carne y adorne con ramitas de perejil.

LASAÑA

1 ½	libras salchichón italiano dulce
2-3	dientes de ajo
½	taza de cebolla picada
½	taza de pimiento rojo, picado
4-6	onzas champiñones frescos rebanados
2	cucharadas de perejil fresco, picado
2	cucharadas de albahaca fresca, picada
2	cucharadas de orégano, picado sal y pimienta al gusto
1	lata de pasta de tomate de 6 onzas
1	lata grande de tomates enteros
1	lata de salsa de tomate de 8 onzas
1 ½	tazas de agua
2	envases de queso "ricotta"
2	huevos batidos ligeramente
1	taza de queso parmesano fresco, rallado
1	cucharadita de sal
¼	cucharadita de pimienta
2	cucharadas de perejil fresco, picado
1	libra queso "mozzarella", rebanado
	hojas de lasaña, cocidas

Dore el salchichón (usando un poco de aceite de oliva) y añada el ajo picado, la cebolla, el chile pimiento y los champiñones. Una vez dorados, añada el perejil, el orégano, la sal y la pimienta. Añada la pasta de tomate y deje que se caliente totalmente. Añada la lata de tomates con todo y el jugo y el agua y deje cocer. Haga el relleno de queso. Mezcle el queso "ricotta", los huevos, el queso parmesano, sal, pimienta y perejil. Forme la lasaña en un recipiente para el horno de 16 x 12 poniendo una capa de hojas de lasaña, una capa de la mezcla de quesos, una capa de mozzarella y otra capa de la carne en ese orden. Repita el proceso. Hornee al descubierto a 350 grados por 30 minutos. Puede congelarse, pero debe congelarse antes de hornear.

TORTELLINI AL HORNO CON BERENJENA Y PAPA

½ libra berenjena, en rebanadas de ¾"
½ libra tortellini rellenos de carne o queso
½ libra papas, peladas y cortadas en rebanadas de ¾"
½ taza de aceite de oliva
1 lata de tomatos a la italiana de 14 ½ onzas
½ cucharadita de orégano fresco, picado
una pizca de pimienta de Cayena
una pizca de sal y de pimienta resca molida
1 taza de queso "Fontina", rallado (puede substituirse por mozzarella)
2 cucharadas de orégano o perejil frescos, picado

Caliente el horno a 375 grados. Rocíe la berenjena con la sal y déjela escurrir en un colador en la pileta de la cocina. Hierva los tortellini, escurra y coloque en un recipiente para horno extendido. En una cacerola pequeña, hierva las papas hasta que queden apenas cocidas. Escurra. Caliente un poco de aceite en una sartén y dore las papas. Vacíe con los tortellini. Con un poco más de aceite, dore suavemente la cebolla por cinco minutos, y añada la berenjena escurrida. Continúe cociendo, añadiendo más aceite de ser necesario, hasta que la berenjena quede tierna y dorada. Drene ligeramente los tomates y añada a la cacerola, rompiéndolos con una cucharada de madera. Añada el orégano, la pimienta de Cayena, la sal y la pimienta. Cocine de cinco a diez minutos más o hasta que el líquido de los tomates se haya reducido y solo quede muy poco. Añada a los tortellini y revuelva con un tercio del queso. Sasone con sal y pimienta. Cubra con el resto del queso y rocíe con el orégano o el perejil restantes. Hornee por 10 minutos o hasta que se derrita el queso y se le formen burbujas.

Rinde: 4 porciones

CORDERO DE CELEBRACION

5	libras pierna de cordero
	sal
	pimienta
	orégano
2	dientes de ajo (pelados y cortados en rebanadas gruesas)
¼	taza de mantequilla, fundida
	jugo de un limón grande
1	cebolla grande picada
1	taza de champiñones rebanados
1	taza de agua

Caliente el horno a 500 grados. Coloque el cordero, con el lado de la piel hacia arriba, en una charola de hornear al descubierto. Unte con sal, pimienta y orégano. Usando la punta de un cuchillo afilado, haga cortes al cordero y rellenélos con las rebanadas de ajo. Añada las cebollas, los champiñones y la mitad del agua. Ponga a hornear por 20 minutos. Añada el resto del agua. Baje la temperatura del horno a 350 grados y hornee hasta que se cueza, bañándolo ocasionalmente. Sirva con arroz cocido.

CERDO Y CALABAZAS

2	libras chuletas, o espaldilla de cerdo
1	cebolla rebanada
1	diente de ajo, aplanado
1	lata de granos de maíz
3	ramitas de cilantro
1	tomate en cubos
6	calabacitas tiernas,rebanadas
	agua
	pizca de comino

Dore el cerdo hasta que esté cocido a medias. Añada la cebolla, el ajo, los granos de maíz, el cilantro y dore a fuego lento. Añada la calabaza, un poco de agua y el comino y cocine hasta que la calabaza quede tierna.

Rinde: 4-6 porciones

POLLO CON PASTA Y TOMATES SECADOS AL SOL

¼	taza de aceite de olivo
3	pechugas de pollo grandes, deshuesadas, cortadas en cubos de 1 pulgada
1	cebolla, picada
1	diente de ajo, picado
½	cucharadita de semilla de hinojo[7]
1	zanahoria, pelada y cortada en tiras
¼	taza de tomates secados al sol en aceite, picados
12	onzas fettucine pasta, recién hervida
1	taza de queso parmesano fresco, rallado

7 *Hinojo - "Fennel"*

Caliente el aceite en una cacerola grande de fondo grueso sobre calor medio. Añada el pollo y cocine por cerca de seis minutos hasta que esté dorado y bien cocido por dentro. Usando una espumadera o cuchara con ranuras, saque el pollo y coloque en un tazón grande. Mantenga caliente. Añada la cebolla, el ajo y las semillas de hinojo a la sartén y cocine hasta que las cebollas estén tiernas. Añada la zanahoria y los tomates secados al sol, y siga cocinando hasta que la zanahoria esté dorada y suave, removiendo ocasionalmente. Vacíe al tazón con el pollo. Añada la pasta y el queso parmesano y revuelva ligeramente. Sirva inmediatamente.

Rinde: 4 porciones

POLLO CON ALCACHOFAS Y TOMATES

4	pechugas de pollo deshuesadas harina sasonada con especias
¾	taza de caldo de pollo
¾	taza de vino blanco
1	lata de corazones de alcachofa
1	lata de tomates
5	cebollitas de Cambray, "cebollines" picadas
½	pimiento verde, picado

Revuelva el pollo en la harina sasonada hasta cubrir por todos lados. Dore lentamente en el aceite, cerca de 10-15 minutos. Baje el fuego, añada el vino y el caldo de pollo. Cubra y cocine por 30 minutos. Añada las alcachofas, la cebolla, el pimiento verde y los tomates. Cocine por 5 o 10 minutos más. Sirva con arroz.

LINGUINI CON POLLO AL HORNO

1	paquete de linguini de 12 onzas
1	pollo entero
2	latas chicas de leche evaporada
2	latas de crema de pollo
1	barra de mantequilla
	queso cheddar o colby

Hierva el pollo en agua por 30 minutos. Cuando esté cocido, saque el pollo y conserve el caldo. Hierva el linguini en el caldo de pollo siguiendo las instrucciones en la envoltura. Deshuese el pollo y corte en trozos pequeños. Mezcle la leche evaporada, la crema de pollo y la mantequilla fundida en un tazón. Añada el pollo y el linguini. Vacíe en un molde para hornear de 9"x13" y cubra con queso. Hornee a 350 grados de 20 a 30 minutos o hasta que forme burbujas. Opcional: añada cebollas doradas y champiñones, sal de ajo y pimienta de Cayena para dar mas sabor.

POLLO CORDON BLEU

4	pechugas de pollo sin piel, deshuesadas, aplanadas muy delgadas
4	porciones de queso suizo, rebanado muy fino
4	porciones de jamón, rebanado muy fino
½	taza de harina
1 ½	tazas de migajas de pan, sasonadas
1-2	huevos batidos
½	taza de aceite
1	paquete de salsa de champiñones en polvo Knorr
½	libra champiñones, rebanados
1	cucharada de mantequilla
1	taza de crema
⅔	taza de vino blanco seco
¼	taza de queso suizo, rallado

Coloque las rebanadas de jamón y de queso sobre el pollo. Enrolle firmemente y asegure con un palillo de dientes. Repita el proceso con todas las pechugas. Revuelva los rollos de pollo muy bien en harina para cubrirlos totalmente. Remoje en el huevo. Cubra totalmente con las migajas de pan. Caliente el aceite en una sartén con revestimiento antiadherible. Fría los rollos de pollo en la sartén por aproximadamente 20 minutos, volteando ocasionalmente hasta que estén dorados. Coloque en un recipiente para hornear de 16"x9" y hornee cubierto a 350 grados por 15 minutos. Saque y añada la salsa de champiñones. Hornee de nuevo por 30 minutos. Saque el molde y retire la cubierta. Hornee por 10 minutos.

Salsa de champiñones:
Mezcle la salsa en polvo, los champiñones, la mantequilla, la crema, el vino y el queso suizo en una sartén a fuego mediano. Cocine por media hora hasta que esté bien caliente.

POLLO BON APPETITE

2   pollos para freir de 4 a 5 libras cortados en piezas y sin piel
1   barra de mantequilla o margarina
2   cebollas, rebanadas
¾   taza de "sherry" (vino Jerez)
½   taza de jugo de tomate
1   lata de salsa de tomate de 8 onzas
2   cucharaditas de paprika
1   cucharadita de sal
½   cucharadita de glutamato monosódico
1   taza de agua caliente o de caldo de pollo

Ponga a freir el pollo en una sartén hasta que quede ligeramente dorado. Saque y coloque en un recipiente para hornear. En la sartén cocine las cebollas hasta que queden amarillas. Añada los ingredientes restantes hasta que llegue a hervir. Vacíe sobre el pollo. Hornee a 400 grados por 30 minutos. Sirva con arroz.

CEBOLLAS AL HORNO CON VINAGRE DE FRAMBUESA[8]

4   cebollas medianas "1015"
1   cucharada de mantequilla
2   cucharadas de vinagre de frambuesa
2   cucharadas de azúcar
1-4 taza de agua

[8] *Frambuesa - "Raspberry"*

Pele las cebollas, cortando lo menos posible la parte de las raíces. Pongalas a remojar en agua hirviendo y déjelas en el agua por cinco o diez minutos, dependiendo de su tamaño. Drene. Cuando se hayan enfriado lo suficiente para manejarse, corte a la mitad y coloque en un platón para hornear, con la parte del corte hacia abajo. Disuelva el azúcar en el vinagre de frambuesa y el agua y vacíe sobre las cebollas. Corte la mantequilla y coloque encima. Hornee a 350 grados de 30 a 40 minutos, bañando frecuentemente hasta que queden tiernas.
Rinde: 4 porciones

PAN DE MAIZ CON BROCOLI

2   barras de mantequilla
4   huevos, bien batidos
1   taza de queso "cottage", de
    cuajada pequeña
1   manojo de cebollitas de
    Cambray, "cebollino"
1   paquete de brócoli congelado
    de 10 onzas, descongelado
½   cucharadita de azúcar
2   sobres de Jiffy Corn de
    8.5 onzas
½   taza de queso cheddar

Dore rápidamente las cebollas en ¼ de la margarina. Mezcle todos los ingredientes y vacíe en un molde para horno engrasado de 9"x13". Hornee a 350 grados por 35 minutos o hasta que la parte de arriba se dore ligeramente.

ENVUELTOS DE EJOTE

1   libra de ejotes cocidos
6   rebanadas de tocino crudo
½   taza de azúcar morena o
    mascabado, firmemente
    comprimida
¾   barra de mantequilla
    polvo de ajo
    sal y piemienta al gusto

Corte el tocino por la mitad. Divida los ejotes en doce envueltos amarrando con las rebanadas de tocino y asegurando con un palillo de dientes. Coloque en un molde de hornear plano. En una sartén funda la mantequilla y añada el azúcar moreno y los condimientos. Vacíe sobre los envueltos. Hornee cubierto a 350 grados por 35 minutos, bañándolos después de los primeros 15 minutos. Retire la cubierta y hornee por 10 minutos más.

ESPARRAGOS CON TOMATES FRESCOS Y ENELDO

1	libra espárragos frescos
1	cucharada de aceite de oliva
½	cebolla, finamente picada
4	dientes de ajos, picaditos
3	tomates frescos, finamente picados
1	manojo de eneldo fesco, picado
¼	taza de vino blanco
2	cucharadas de mantequilla

En agua hirviendo vivamente, sumerga los espárragos rápidamente. Deje cocer de 2 a 3 minutos. Drene en un colador y coloque inmediatamente los espárragos en agua helada. Esto mantendrá el color de los espárragos verde brillante. Si el agua no está helada el color de los espárragos se torna café. En una sartén, añada 1 cucharada de aceite de oliva. Cuando el aceite se haya calentado, añada las cebollas picadas y fría por dos minutos. Añada el ajo y fría rápidamente por un minuto más. Añada el tomate, el eneldo y el vino blanco y deje que el líquido se espese por tres minutos. Baje el fuego y añada la mantequilla, para que la salsa se espese ligeramente. No deje que hierva. Sirva la salsa sobre los espárragos.

Rinde: 4-6 porciones

SOPA DE CAMARONES CREOLE

1 ½	libras camarón, pelado y desvenado
½	taza de margarina, mantequilla o aceite de cocina
¼	taza de harina
1	taza de cebolla, picada
½	taza de apio, picado
1	diente de ajo, picado finamente
2	latas de caldo de pollo, de bajo contenido de sodio
1	lata de tomate en trozo de 28 onzas, drenada
½	taza de vino blanco
2	cucharadas de perejil, picado
1	cucharada de jugo de limón
1	hoja de laurel
½	cucharadita de sal
¼	cucharadita de pimienta de Cayena
¼	cucharadita de azafrán

En una olla para caldo grande derrita la mantequilla o la margarina a fuego mediano. Prepare la salsa moviendo constantemente y añadiendo lentamente la harina. Siga moviendo hasta que la mezcla esté tersa y con un ligero color café. Añada la cebolla, el apio y el ajo y continúe moviendo hasta que los ingredientes estén suaves. Añada el caldo de pollo gradualmente. Añada los ingredientes restantes, excepto el camarón. Deje que hierva y cocine a fuego lento por diez minutos. Añada el camarón y cocine por cinco minutos más o hasta que el camarón adquiera un color rosado y se haya cocido.

Rinde: 6 porciones

Led by Dianne Brumley, conductor and artistic director, the South Texas Chorale is made up of seventy-five volunteer vocalists. The group has received State recognition and their five annual performaces are great favorites with "Winter Texans" as well as a source of civic pride for local citizens. In a few short years, their Christmas program has become a family holiday tradition.

SOPA DE MAIZ AL ESTILO SOUTHWEST

4	tazas de dientes de maíz crudo
1	pimiento rojo, rebanado
¼	taza de cebolla, picada
2	cucharadas de mantequilla
2	cucharadas de harina
	sal y pimienta al gusto
2	tazas de caldo de pollo
2	tazas de leche
1	taza de queso cheddar, rallado
1	lata de rebanadas de chile verde de 4 onzas
1	taza de tocino, frito, en trocitos
	tortillas de maíz fritas partidas en trozo o "tortilla chips"

Fría el maíz, el pimiento rojo y la cebolla en la mantequilla hasta que estén cocidos. Añada la harina, la sal y la pimienta y cocine por un minuto. Añada gradualmente el caldo de pollo, y la leche, alternando hasta que la mezcla se espese. Añada el queso cheddar, los chiles verdes y la mitad del tocino. Tenga cuidado de no sobrecalentar. Sirva en tazones individuales con trozos de tortilla. Adorne con el resto del tocino y las rebanadas de pimiento rojo.

ENSALADA DE MANGO

3	paquetes de gelatina de limón de 3 onzas
3	tazas de agua hirviendo
1	paquete de queso crema de 8 onzas
1	lata o frasco de mangos de 26 onzas
1	taza de jugo de mango
1	taza de crema agria
3-4	cucharadas de miel de abeja

Disuelva la gelatina en el agua hirviendo. En una licuadora, combine el queso crema, los mangos y el jugo de mango. Vacíe algo de la mezcla de gelatina hasta que la licuadora se llene. Mezcle. Vacíe el licuado en un tazón con el resto de la mezcla de gelatina y revuelva bien. Vacíe en un molde engrasado y refrigere hasta que quede firme. Combine la crema agria y la miel hasta que estén bien mezclados. Rocíe sobre la ensalada cuando esté lista para servirse.

POSTRE DE PISTACHE

1	caja de budín de pistache en polvo (pudding)
1	envase de "Cool Whip" de 9 onzas
1	lata de piña en trozos de 20 onzas
¾	taza de malvaiscos pequeños

Mezcle todos los ingredientes muy bien y refrigere por 2 horas.

ENSALADA DE PAN DE MAIZ

2	paquetes de harina de maiz con jalapeño
1	manojo de cebollitas de Cambray, "cebollines", picadas
1	pimiento verde, picado
2	tomates, picados
1	lata de granos de maíz de 16 onzas, drenados
1	taza de queso cheddar fuerte, rallado
8	rebanadas de tocino, fritas y en trocitos
1 ½	tazas de mayonesa
½	taza de crema agria
½	cucharadita de chile en polvo
	pimienta al gusto
	rebanadas de aguacate para adornar

Prepare el pan de maíz siguiendo las instrucciones en la envoltura. Enfríe y parta en pedazos en un tazón. Añada los demás ingredientes, excepto el aguacate. Revuelva bien y refrigere por lo menos 8 horas. Adorne con aguacates.

POLLO Y ENSALADA DE AGUACATE
CON ADEREZO DE TOCINO

2   latas de caldo de pollo
6   pechugas de pollo, deshuesadas y sin piel, en mitades
2   aguacates, en cuadritos y revueltos en dos cucharaditas de jugo de limón
½   taza de cebollitas de Cambray, picadas
½   libra tocino
1   huevo grande, a temperatura ambiente
5   cucharaditas de jugo de limón fresco
1   cucharadita de mostaza tipo "Dijon"
¼   cucharadita de sal
¼   cucharadita de pimienta blanca
½   taza de aceite vegetal

En una sartén, caliente el caldo de pollo hasta que hierva y añada las pechugas de pollo. Reduzca la temperatura y cocine, volteando las pechugas hasta que estén cocidas. Quite la sartén del fuego y deje el pollo en el caldo hasta que se enfríe por 30 minutos. Para preparar el aderezo, cocine el tocino hasta que esté dorado y crujiente y drene la grasa. Reserve ¼ de taza de la grasa de tocino y deje enfriar por 15 minutos. En un procesador de alimentos o licuadora, mezcle el huevo, el jugo de limón, la mostaza, la sal y la pimienta blanca. Mientras se revuelve lentamente vacíe la grasa del tocino y el aceite vegetal vertiendo en un chorro contínuo. Añada el tocino y mezcle por cinco segundos. Corte el pollo en cubos. En un tazón, combine el pollo, el aguacate, las cebollitas de Cambray y revuelva cuidadosamente con el aderezo. Sirva inmediatamente.

ENSALADA DE ESPINACA
DE INVIERNO

1   libra espinaca, lavada, secada y partida en pedazos

1   cebolla roja, en rebanadas muy delgadas

8   rebanadas de tocino, fritas y en trocitos

    una pizca de pimienta

4   huevos duros, picados

1   lata de castaña de agua

¼   libra champiñones, rebanados

½   taza de queso suizo rebanado

1   taza de aceite

⅓   taza de vinagre de sidra

½   taza de azúcar

1   cucharadita de cebolla seca en trocitos

½   cucharadita de pimentón (paprika)

½   cucharadita de mostaza seca

Refrigere los primeros ocho ingredientes. Mezcle el aceite, el vinagre, el azúcar, la cebolla, la paprika y la mostaza seca en un recipiente cerrado y sacuda vigorosamente. Justo antes de servir, mezcle los ingredientes de la ensalada juntos y revuelva con el aderezo.

CREPAS DE ESPARRAGOS Y HIERBAS DE OLOR

1 ½ tazas de harina, cernida
1   taza de leche
1   taza de agua
4   huevos
     pizca de sal
     pizca de nuez moscada, recién
     rallada
½   barra de mantequilla sin sal,
     fundida
1   cucharada de perejil de hoja
     plana, finamente picado
1   cucharada de cebollinos,
     finamente picados
1   cucharada de eneldo fresco,
     finamente picado
1   cucharadita de mantequilla

Relleno:
1   libra queso tipo Brie
4   onzas queso Roquefort
6   cucharadas de mantequilla sin
     sal, a la temperatura ambiente
½   taza de crema para batir
     pimienta blanca recién molida
20-25 espárragos frescos, cocidos alvapor,
     y enfriados en refrigeración

Combine, la harina, la leche, el agua, los huevos, la sal y la nuez moscada en una licuadora y mezcle hasta que esté suave. Vacíe en un tazón para batir. Añada la mantequilla derretida y las hierbas de olor y revuelva hasta qaue estén bien incorporadas, Cubra y deje reposar dos horas a la temperatura ambiente para que los sabores se combinen. Caliente la cucharadita de mantequilla en una sartén para sabores se combinen. Caliente la cucharadita de mantequilla en una sartén para crepas de 6". Añada justamente la mantequilla necesaria para cubrir el fondo de la sartén y deje que cada crepa se dore ligeramente por ambos lados. Repita con la mezcla restante, añadiendo más mantequilla de ser necesario.

En un procesador combine el queso y la mantequilla, y mezcle usado seis ciclos de encendido-apagado. Añada crema y pimienta y mezcle hasta que esté completamente suave. Cubra y deje reposar a la temperatura ambiente una hora antes de servir.

Para preparar las crepas coloque un espárrago en el centro de cada crepa. Ponga el relleno en una dulla y ponga el relleno a lo largo del espárrago. Enrolle la crepa como una tortilla.

CANAPES DE CANGREJO Y QUESO

1 taza de queso para untar
1 libra de carne de cangrejo, fresca
  o de lata
¼ taza de mantequilla, suavizada
1 cucharada de mayonesa
½ cucharadita de sal o sasonador
¼ cucharadita de sal de ajo
10 panecillos tipo English muffin

Combine los primeros seis ingredientes. Mezcle bien. Unte generosamente en cada mitad del muffin. Corte cada mitad en cuartos. Coloque en charolas par ahornear y dore por cinco minutos. Pueden colocarse a dorar estando congelados.

PAN RELLENO SORRENTO

2 hogazas de pan francés
3 rebanadas de tocino
12 onzas queso suizo, rallado
2 manojos de cebollitas de
  Cambray
2 barras de mantequilla en
  rebanadas

Parta las hogazas a la mitad, a lo largo, pero no corte totalmente. Coloque todos los ingredientes entre las dos mitades, excepto por una de las barras de mantequilla, que puede usarse para cubrir las hogazas. Envuelva en papel aluminio y caliente en el horno a 350 grados por 20 minutos o hata que el queso se haya fundido.

RELLENO DE JAMON Y QUESO
PARA SANDWICH

1 libra tocino, frito, escurrido y
  en trocitos
2 tazas de queso Cheddar, rallado
½ taza de almendras en jojuelas,
  tostadas
1 taza de mayonesa
2 cucharadas de cebollitas de
  Cambray, picadas

Mezcle todos los ingredientes e incorpore bien. Unte sobre el pan y haga un sandwich. Corte las orillas, corte en cuartos y sirva.

DIP DE CAMARON ESTILO SOUTH TEXAS

1	taza de camarones, cocidos y picaditos
1	paquete de 8 onzas de queso crema, suavizado
¼	taza de cebollitas de Cambray (ambas partes blancas y verdes), picaditas
¼	de taza de aceitunas rellenas de jalapeño (o aceitunas normales y jalapeños en vinagre)
¼	taza de mayonesa ligera o aderezo para ensaladas tipo Ranch
¼	cucharadita de sal o sasonador
¼	cucharadita de pimienta negra

Combine todos los ingredientes y mezcle bien. Adorne con más aceitunas picadas. Rinde dos tazas.

INDEX

R

S

ORDER FORM

Name

Address

City

Home phone

No. of copies	@ $18.95 ea.	
Texas residents, add $1.56 sales tax	
Shipping and handling $3.00 ea.	
Total	

Check enclosed ☐
(payable to the Junior League of Harlingen)

Please charge to:
Mastercard ☐   VISA ☐

Card number: _____

Expiration date: _____

Signature: _____

To open a wholesale account, call 210.425.5690

The Junior League of Harlingen, Texas
P.O. Box 1726
Harlingen, Texas 78551
210.425.5690
E-Mail: rio-riches@harlingen.juniorleague.org
http://harlingen.juniorleague.org/harlingen/

ORDER FORM

Name

Address

City

Home phone

No. of copies	@ $18.95 ea.	
Texas residents, add $1.56 sales tax	
Shipping and handling $3.00 ea.	
Total	

Check enclosed ☐
(payable to the Junior League of Harlingen)

Please charge to:
Mastercard ☐   VISA ☐

Card number: _____

Expiration date: _____

Signature: _____

To open a wholesale account, call 210.425.5690

The Junior League of Harlingen, Texas
P.O. Box 1726
Harlingen, Texas 78551
210.425.5690
E-Mail: rio-riches@harlingen.juniorleague.org
http://harlingen.juniorleague.org/harlingen/